CAUGHT
UP IN
CHRIST

To Lori~
My friend
in Christ!

Spiritual First-Aid
for Believers and Seekers

Rick Merfeld

RIVER BIRCH PRESS

Daphne, Alabama

Caught Up in Christ: Spiritual First Aid for Believers and Seekers
by Rick Merfeld
Copyright ©2020 Rick Merfeld

Unless otherwise identified, Scripture is taken from the New American Bible, Revised Edition, Devore and Sons, Inc., Wichita, Kansas. 2011.

ISBN 978-1-951561-11-6 (print)
ISBN 978-1-951561-16-1 (ebook)
For Worldwide Distribution
Printed in the U.S.A.

River Birch Press
P.O. Box 868
Daphne, AL 36526

Contents

To my wife, Dagmar,
and our three sons,
Erick, Eli, and Ehren…
for giving me grace and space
to change and grow

Introduction

Can you feel it—the heartbeat of a country out of rhythm...
the heart of churches throbbing in crisis...a friend or family
member who can feel their heart pounding at the sight of a spiritual wound. Perhaps you have been searching your heart for any
feeling at all and are ready to give up and surrender to the numb-
ness of a flat-lined faith life.

We wake each morning to a world that is more and more anti-
God and anti-Christian. Confusion and fear runs rampant in our
emotionally charged, hyper sexualized, me-driven society.
Unanswered questions lead to doubt and, if left unchecked, mature
into total disbelief. People hear about the latest mass shooting and
stand by utterly dismayed and perplexed by the increasing presence
of evil in our world. With everything going on in our country,
around the world, in our homes, and in our hearts, should we be
surprised that many of us are in need of spiritual first aid?

In these trying and revealing times, you may have doubts but
continue to attend church because it has been the center of your
spirituality for years. As the world around you questions the very
existence of God, holding true to your beliefs may be getting
harder. My Roman Catholic sisters and brothers may find it harder
to hold true to church doctrine. If you are not sure that Christ died
and rose from the dead, it will be hard to believe that He is present
in the Sacraments.

You may be part of a second or third generation of families
who have been enjoying beautiful and meaningful fellowship in
your church since the doors opened, but you fear your faith is
empty. You may have been born into a Catholic family and survived twelve years of Catholic education but have not been to
church since your high school graduation. You may have walked
away from church and no longer believe in God, period.

You might be at the other end of the spectrum and still believe
in God and have a fulfilling personal relationship with Jesus Christ

but are fearful of the failing faith of family and friends. Perhaps you are one of those who have been hurt by a member of the clergy or a pastoral minister or others. You may also be a newly confirmed member of the faith and wonder what all the fuss is about.

Perhaps you are a member of the clergy or a non-Catholic Christian concerned for your Catholic family and friends. You see them hurting, angry, confused, and searching for answers but are unsure about how to care for them.

This book is for all of us. Our faith is about Christ reaching out to us with a life-giving and life-changing relationship with the one, true, living God. Jesus Christ is the foundation of the Christian faith and the cornerstone of Catholicism. This book will encourage you to get caught up in the grace and mercy of Christ, not fear and despair; caught up in the qualities of Christ, not the elements of church; caught up in clarity and not confusion; caught up in healing, not hurt.

We will go beyond the warm and fuzzy metaphysical discussions about heaven and the intriguing debate about hell. Faith must be more than a pass card to the streets of gold or simple fire insurance against the flames of hell. We will go beyond the simple tips and tricks of Christianity and talk about a faith that can generate a measurable difference in how you experience the world and how the world experiences you.

The singular goal of this book is to invite you into a conversation that will impart spiritual first aid, uncover evidence, answer questions, and help you set or reset your faith firmly on the foundation of Christ. How we traverse our todays and transition into any tomorrows does not depend on how many times we genuflect in sacred spaces. However, it does depend on our inviting God into our heart, professing that Jesus Christ is Lord and Savior, and living out the full extent of the Gospel message. I invite you to join me now as we get caught up in Christ.

1

Jesus Among Other Voices
Fighting for Faith in a Noisy World

Have you ever watched a dog chase a rabbit in a field? The dog turns right and left, jumps over fences and runs under trees, trying to catch the rabbit. It's a crazy scene but it makes sense. Take the rabbit out of the picture. The scene no longer makes sense, and the dog just looks crazy. Many people think Christians are crazy. They don't see the rabbit we're chasing.

Our world can be a noisy place. Many voices call out to us about what matters, offering explanations for what is happening around us, giving answers to our questions and solutions for our pain, and promising vastly different versions of peace, pure thoughts, and power. Voices will tell you to set aside faith in anything larger than self and encourage you to pursue your every desire. It's hard to escape the influx of perspectives and belief systems that differ from the Christian worldview.

There have always been voices declaring that God is dead

and that the Jesus story is a bunch of nonsense. Today, however, these voices are ever-present, boisterous, aggressive, and even oppressive. Combine all these voices with the issues facing the church, and you have a great recipe for a modern-day exodus. This time, however, the exodus is not people moving toward God; it's people moving away from God.

Once Christianity was the predominant way of thinking in our country, but those days are gone. In our diverse society no single, dominant worldview now exists. Many beneficial and beautiful elements exist in our pluralistic culture. However, we also need to recognize along with the rich histories, cultural distinctions, and a bountiful harvest of great tasting food, we are also presented with many different spiritual and a-spiritual voices.

We can no longer assume that people believe in God and know the story of Jesus, the Nazarean. Is this an isolated phenomenon or are there other ideas in flux around us? Our parents and grandparents would have never guessed that self-identified socialists would campaign to be the president of the United States. Members of the older generations think of a "45" as a small, plastic record for playing their favorite music while younger readers think it's a handgun used for killing innocent people. Everything seems to be changing. Come on! The Cubs even won a World Series!

Because Jesus is but one voice among many, spiritual first-responders need to meet people where they are and be ready to start with the basics. Vince Lombardi, the legendary football coach of the Green Bay Packers, was known for starting every year with the same simple lesson. He would gather his players around and declare, "Gentlemen, this is a football."[1] As we engage in spiritual first aid, we too need to start with the basics about the faith: what lies at the heart of our faith is the person and deity of Jesus Christ.

There are, however, many voices that deny the revelation of Jesus Christ. Perhaps you've heard some of them: "The Jesus story is just a myth;" "We all worship the same God, so Jesus doesn't matter;" "Jesus was a good teacher, but he didn't die on the cross and rise from the dead;" "It might be true for you, but it's not true for me." These voices openly denounce Christ. There are quiet and deceptive voices too. Let me explain.

I love music. I remember learning about the Pandora music service with great excitement. There are other similar music services available in the market now, but I understand they all work about the same. You enter a song, musician, or type of music that you want to listen to, and you are immediately served up a selection. You sit back and enjoy your favorite tunes as Pandora becomes your own personal jukebox! (Younger readers may need to Google that!)

Over the first few months, I created "stations" dedicated to 80's rock and roll, show tunes, John Denver, and instrumental movie themes, to name a few. I thought I had my love of music by the tail! But then I learned a disturbing feature of the service. I would start off listening to powerful movie themes by John Williams and before I knew it, I was listening to country music! I learned that I had to use the buttons on the screen to like or dislike a certain song. If I didn't stay in charge of what I was listening to, I would be carried off on a musical train that was going in a totally different direction than I had intended.

We need to guard against this Pandora effect as we encounter different voices. If we are not careful, we'll start off in pursuit of our Christ-centered faith and find out later that we are tied into beliefs, views, and even behaviors that are not in keeping with the teachings of Christ and the Word of God. For example, have you heard about the Progressive Christian movement? For people who identify as Christian and also tend to be progressive in their political views, this might sound like a great thing. After all, they profess to believe in Jesus, but (watch for the Pandora effect) also declare that He is only one of the many ways to experience the sacredness of life.

They also believe that you find grace in the search for understanding and believe there is more value in questions than in answers.[2] Jesus made the bold statement that He is the way, truth, and life. He didn't claim to be one of the ways, but THE way. Wouldn't this make the Progressive Christian movement non-Christian?

Surrounded by societal cries for inclusivity, should we be surprised that the world has a problem with the exclusivity of Christ? Winston Churchill once said, "The truth is so valuable that it should be surrounded by a bodyguard of lies."[3] With so many different voices in our ears, what are we to do? How do we know to whom we should listen? Is there an authoritative voice we can turn to?

Roman Catholics have historically tuned into the voice of the Church. But one of the consequences of the Church's turmoil has been a decreasing level of loyalty to and confidence in its leadership and teaching. About a year ago, our parish invited members to attend listening sessions to express their concerns in light of the latest wave of abuse allegations. Parish staff and diocesan leaders were aware that people were grumbling, concerned, and even in crisis over the persistent problem.

The ongoing allegations have even eroded confidence in the extra-ordinary status of the ordained. Church doctrine includes belief about papal infallibility in certain situations, but I would argue that priests, in general, have often been thought of as having special status or special authority. Part of the world's response to the abuse scandal is an outcry that priests are men first, flawed human beings, just like the rest of us. All of this raises doubts and leaves many people looking outside the Church for answers.

What about our confidence in the voice of our education system? One Sunday evening during a recent Easter season, our seven-year-old granddaughter told us what she had learned about Jesus the previous week. "Jesus lived, died, rose from the dead, and is dead again." After a quick chuckle, I began to wonder. Was this simply her way of understanding the Easter story at her developmental stage, or was she re-peating what she had heard from one of the voices at school?

I reached out to her teacher. She received me graciously, and I walked away from our conversation feeling that our little girl was in good hands, in general. However, I remained concerned about what was being taught about God's Word. As we talked about God's Word, the teacher informed me that she had been taught in college that many of the stories in the Bible are just that—stories. The teacher explained that the story of Adam and Eve is just a story, and the great flood never really happened. She believed that the stories were helpful in teaching us things about God and who Jesus is, but that the stories themselves are not true.

The teacher was open to further conversation, so we dis-cussed evidence for the biblical stories and compared them with the alternative secular explanations for things like the genesis of life. If we believe that certain stories in the Bible are just stories, who gets to decide which ones are true and which ones are just stories? And if some stories are not true, do we also get to determine if some of the teachings of Jesus are untrue? The teacher walked away from our conversation questioning what she thought was true. I walked away wondering what our granddaughter and her classmates would learn next in class.

Many voices in our world today can easily bring us to doubt the truth about the Triune God, but just as many voices exist that can bring us to a solid, supported, and secure faith in God the Father, Christ the Son, and the ever-present Holy Spirit.

At the heart of the faith is the Sacred Heart of Jesus. Either Jesus is who He says He is, or He is not. C.S. Lewis wrote that everyone who considers Christ will come to one of three conclusions about Jesus: He is either a liar, a lunatic, or Lord.[4] Is this oversimplifying our faith? Consider what Jesus said as recorded in Mark 10:13-15.

> *The people brought children to Jesus, hoping he might touch them. The disciples rebuked them. When Jesus saw this, He became indignant and said to them, "Let the children come to me. Do not prevent them for the kingdom of God belongs to such as these. Amen I say to you, whoever does not accept God's kingdom like a child will not enter it."*

Could it be that Jesus knew that people would have a tendency to complicate things? Could it be Jesus knew those who stood against Him would only have to complicate things enough to create doubt in the mind of a believer to claim victory? In a courtroom, a defense attorney does not have to prove "who dun it"; the defense attorney only needs to create a reasonable doubt, and the accused goes free. Complications raise doubt. Doubt erodes confidence.

The Judeo-Christian faith has always been a free-market faith where you and I are at liberty to give our love freely to God or withhold it completely. The question that lies before us today is the same question that people have been wrestling with for over 3000 years.

> *Now therefore, fear the Lord, and serve Him in sincerity and in truth; and cast out the gods which your fathers served on the other side of the river and in Egypt, and serve the Lord. If it is displeasing to you to serve the Lord, choose you this day whom you will serve, whether the gods which your fathers served beyond the river, or the gods of the Amorites in whose country you are dwelling. As for me and my household, we will serve the Lord* (Joshua 24: 14-15).

Whom or what will you serve? Whom or what lies at the heart of your spirituality?

I've been journaling now for nearly fifteen years. The first entry was recorded on May 19, 2006. After giving a talk on study at our parish CEW (Christian Experience Weekend), I was invited to join a Living Last Supper Ministry team. The team acts out the Lord's last supper. During the following Lenten Season, I had the honor of being in the role of Jesus. During Mass on Easter morning, I realized how humbling and deeply meaningful that Lenten season had been.

As preparation for the ministry that year, the team read through Rick Warren's *Purpose Driven Life*. Here is that first journal entry: "I am almost finished with *Purpose Driven Life*. It has made a big difference. Warren suggests journaling. Here we go." My journals now chronicle how my life has changed since I took hold of my faith and committed my life to Christ. Each day, I am more and more confident that how we experience the world and how the world experiences us depends on who or what lies at the heart of our spirituality.

Reflection

1. What "voices" are you currently listening to that are informing and shaping your spirituality?

2. The Bible declares "Oh, that today you would hear His voice: Harden not your heart as at the rebellion" (Hebrews 3:15). If God were to speak to you today, would you listen?

3. What impact is the media and social media having on your thinking? Does it create doubts, questions, or confusion for your faith?

2

Imagine the Possibilities
Start with the End in Mind

You will be the same person in five years as you are today except for the people you meet and the books you read. ~Charlie "Tremendous" Jones

The active Christ-centered life calls us forever forward to a more complete awareness of God and into a deeper relationship with Jesus Christ. That sounds good, but what does it mean for our personal experiences and our daily agenda? Is our awareness of God just a Sunday thing and our relationship with Jesus just a Church thing?

This book will illuminate five outcomes you can expect from getting caught up in Christ and the Holy Word of God. We're not talking about superficial tips and tricks but measurable results that you can see and touch, quantifiable outcomes that will change the way you experience the world and how the world experiences you. The five outcomes are an enhanced sense of peace, a powerful partnership, a godly perspective, pure thoughts, and lastly, the life-changing impact

9

of being persuaded by the truth about God and becoming persuasive for His kingdom.

How do we achieve these outcomes for ourselves and help others do the same? Getting caught up in Christ goes beyond the Sunday experience and our involvement with church. If we put God in the Sunday box, we underestimate and even limit His power. And if we recognize the Church as the only authority on our faith, we muffle the voice of Christ.

Questions arise. Do you long for peace of mind? Are there fears that you want to overcome and problems that you would like to solve? Are you searching for a way to make sense of the world and to find your place in it? Can you imagine how your life might be better if you could change the way you impact those around you? Do you long for a way to help those around you to achieve peace and the changes they desire? Can you imagine a deeper, more meaningful worship experience?

If you are like me, you answered yes to one or more of the questions. Look around. People everywhere are searching for answers, and many are finding out the world has over-promised and under-delivered. It's important to start our search by imagining the difference Christ would make in our life and in the lives of our family and friends.

Not everyone feels safe enough to dream those dreams. Many people have been disappointed by life events, unkept promises, and even perceived unanswered prayer. Many are full of doubt. The writer of Hebrews declares that "Faith is the realization of what is hoped for and evidence of things not seen." Providing spiritual first aid requires us to listen to people and seek to understand them. If they are in a safe space where they can imagine things somehow getting better, they will discover and uncover their hidden potential and be gradually open to greater faith, not less.

Unfortunately doubts continually creep into our life. They can trip us up and become stumbling blocks to our faith or even paralyze our progress. The Gospel of Mark speaks to us about a man who had doubts. The man had a son who was possessed by a mute spirit.

> *They brought the boy to Him. And when he saw Him, the spirit immediately threw the boy into convulsions. As he fell to the ground, he began to roll around and foam at the mouth. Then Jesus questioned his father, "How long has this been happening to him?" He replied, "Since childhood. It has often thrown him into fire and into water to kill him. But if you can do anything, have compassion on us and help us." Jesus said to him, "If you can! Everything is possible to one who has faith." Then the boy's father cried out, "I do believe, help my unbelief!" Jesus, on seeing a crowd rapidly gathering, rebuked the unclean spirit and said to it, "Mute and deaf spirit, I command you: come out of him and never enter him again!" Shouting and throwing the boy into convulsions, it came out. He (the boy) became like a corpse, which caused many to say, "He is dead!" But Jesus took him by the hand, raised him, and the boy stood up* (Mark 9: 20-27).

"Help my unbelief," the man said. For many people, the journey toward Christ is about replacing doubt with faith. This can feel like a high-risk proposition. Where does hope live? Hope lives in ever closer proximity to Jesus Christ and risking the thought that things can, indeed, get better..

Before we move forward to the five outcomes, we need to

take a quick look at the spiritual lamppost that will show us the way.

My Discovery of the Bible

The Catholic Church proudly proclaims the Bible is the Word of God. In 1965, Vatican II called for a Bible revival.[5] Have we been successful? Consider what "Word on Fire" founder Bishop Robert Barron noted in 2014.

> The reason Vatican II called for a Biblical revival is that the church's task is primarily to tell the world this great story. The tragedy is that so many of us in the Church have lost a sense of the Bible. When you make Biblical references today, oftentimes people are lost. Our job is to keep the Holy Word of God, to know it so we can announce it to the wider world.[6]

We honor the Bible during Mass as it is lifted up as the sacred Word of God. In their book, *Rebuilt*, authors Fr. Michael White and Tom Corcoran declare:

> Next to the Sacraments, preaching the Word of God is one of the most important things you can do to grow disciples, and it's even more important when it comes to reaching the lost...as well as those new to the discipleship path.[7]

While the "Good Book" is critically important, we might be surprised to discover that we only cover a small portion of the Scriptures during a given year. The Roman Catholic Church rotates through three cycles of essential readings over a three-year period, yet the readings center on the same set of essential events, teachings, and messages.

Have you ever wondered what other stories and messages are found in the Bible? Could they possibly make a real difference in your life? I had a number of Bibles in my home and office, but they were dusty and longed to be noticed and revered. Having attended Mass nearly every weekend for 50 years, I had heard familiar scripture lessons over and over again.

As a young boy, I treasured serving funeral Masses and often heard familiar readings. Holy Week liturgies were steeped in rich stories. In high school, I continued building my faith through retreats where we reflected on Bible parables. But, over time, I learned a great portion of the Bible was simply unknown to me. There were so much more than the few passages that were voiced from the pulpit. I also had no reason to think that I could achieve a more meaningful relationship with Jesus without digging deeper into the Bible.

During my college years, I spent a great deal of time with members of the Lutheran faith. A number of my friends really knew their Bible! For a semester, a great friend of mine attended Wednesday morning Mass with me. He always gave me a hard time about standing, sitting, and kneeling; up, down, up down. We would meet at the dining hall and then he would say, "I am ready for my Wednesday morning calisthenics!" For a couple of college boys, it was good exercise!

I also remember feeling intimidated by my wife's knowledge of the Catholic faith and the scriptures. Dagmar was raised in a Lutheran home and her faith journey included time in a Jewish synagogue where she studied the Old Testament. Some years later, she was confirmed in the Catholic Church. For many years, I shied away from discussions with her about our faith and the Bible because I felt I had very little to offer.

Our marital journey has now lasted 32 years. If passage into heaven were based on good works, she would be a shoe-in having lived with me so long. As our three boys worked their way through junior high school, Dagmar and I began to attend weekend retreats. This was one of the first times I saw the Bible lifted up in a new light. I was challenged to read it for myself.

In all fairness, there were likely earlier times when I was encouraged to do so, but I did not have ears to hear. Around this same time I met Jim, who would become a lifelong mentor and spiritual guide. He constantly pushed me to renew my mind by reading good works, especially the Bible. I cannot overstate the impact this relationship has had on my spirituality and my life.

I was not a reader. Not only did I neglect the Bible, very little time was spent reading anything! After much encouragement, I did begin reading short daily devotionals, and before long, a new book every couple of months. I did begin to see how the new input was shaping my mind and transforming my heart.

I also started reading through the Bible for the first time— Genesis to Revelation. I harvested great joy and surprise, as well as a number of humbling experiences. I remember one experience especially well. My family and I are baseball nuts. I played college ball, and we coached our boys as they passed through kid leagues. A young man played on our team one year, and I got to know him and his family well. They were members of the Morman Church of Latter Day Saints.

We ran into each other a number of years later and rekindled our friendship centered on our faith journeys. He invited me to attend a closed-circuit meeting of their yearly General

Assembly. During the presentation, I heard one of the speakers quote John 10:16. In this verse, Jesus says, "I have other sheep that do not belong to this fold." The speaker cited this as evidence that Jesus foresaw the coming church of the Latter Day Saints.

I was shocked. Did Jesus really say that? I remember racing home to see if that verse was in my Bible too. It was. I had never seen nor heard that verse before. The verse is part of the Good Shepard discourse in the Gospel of John. Christians understand that the "other sheep" are the many Gentiles that will come to faith in Christ in Jesus' time and ours. Humbled by this experience, I wondered what else I was missing.

Great value comes in listening to other people talk about the Bible and hearing their personal insights. I have been blessed by great sermons and Bible studies, speakers and authors. I also believe each of us is called to spend time with God's Word ourselves. Imagine you were removed from your father's home as a baby. As a teenager, you get reunited with your brothers and sisters you never knew. You could learn a lot about your dad from your siblings, but that would never compare with what you would know about your Dad if you had a personal relationship with him!

Reading the Bible reveals the heart of our heavenly Father and moves us forward to an intimate relationship with Jesus Christ. Just like our dads have unique connections with each of their children, God longs for a unique relationship with each of us. My experience reading God's Word is living proof that this personal relationship will change your life as it has mine!

How Do We Know that the Bible Is the Word of God?

In today's world, it is no surprise that many people doubt that the Bible is the inspired and authoritative word of God. If it is anything less than this, could there be any accuracy in its details or power in its content? You may have other questions or perhaps you've heard doubts expressed by those around you, such as does God really exist? Is there any way to know if Jesus really died on a cross at Calvary and rose from the dead?

We wake up each morning to a world that is increasingly hostile to God and the Christian worldview. Unanswered questions lead to doubts; doubts, if unchecked, can mature into total disbelief. I had similar questions and doubts. I thank God that I was also provided with answers.

I was amazed at the great body of evidence that shredded my doubts! It would be crazy to try and cover it all here, but I'll administer a quick shot of facts as first aid. We'll start at the beginning. Scientific discoveries now show definitively that our universe had a beginning.[8] Even the world-renowned atheist scientist Stephen Hawking declares this to be true.[9] And if the universe had a beginning, it had to have a beginner!

What can we know about this beginner? The beginner or creator is spaceless, timeless, immaterial, personal, intelligent, and loving to design our known world. All of these characteristics are consistent with the God of the Bible.[10] If the greatest miracle of all time—the creation of our earthly world—happened on the first page of the Bible, would it be easier to believe that Jesus walked on water and turned water into wine?

I have also been amazed to discover the documented chain of custody, if you will. Evidence exists through which we can trace the books of the New Testament back to the original sources, the authors, people like you and me who walked and talked with Jesus. There are books that are not included in the Bible, in part, because there is no chain of custody that traces the work to verifiable, original sources.

What about the Old Testament books? Can we have faith in their reliability and authority? Yes. We know the Old Testament books are credible because of archaeological evidence and because Jesus quoted Old Testament scripture as did St. Paul, St. Peter, and other New Testament writers.[11]

For example, in chapter 5 of this book, we're going to recall one of the epic spiritual contests of all time. It's the story of the prophet Elijah and his contest with the Baal gods on Mount Carmel. The story is told in 1 Kings 18. In his letter to the Romans (Romans 11:2-4), St. Paul recalls this same event and specifically mentions how Elijah pleaded with God after the contest. We read about this event today, the same event that St. Paul wrote about in the year 57 A.D, over 2000 years ago! St. Paul placed his faith on Old Testament scripture. We can too!

There is a boat load of evidence on which the Christian faith rests. Does evidence impact your level of belief? Do our statements of faith become more credible when we can answer questions and handle objections? Jesus, Himself, recognized the value of evidence when standing up for the faith.

When John (the Baptist) heard in prison of the works of the Messiah, he sent his disciples to Him with this question: "Are you the one who is to come, or should we look for another?" Jesus said to them in reply, "Go and tell John what you hear and see: the blind regain their sight, the dead are raised, and the poor have the good news proclaimed to them. And blessed is the one who takes no offense at me" (Matthew 11: 2-6).

Today, especially today, non-believers and believers as well, hunger for evidence that makes it easier to hold fast to the truth about Christ as revealed in the natural world and in the Holy Bible. The world may mock those who are caught up in Christ. Yet, evidence answers questions, dissolves doubt, and empowers faith.

Reflection

1. How confident are you in the evidence for God and the deity of Jesus Christ? Where do you currently have questions and doubts?

2. If someone were to ask you if the Bible is the inspired and authoritative Word of God, how would you respond?

3. When pursuing a relationship with Christ, you can anticipate changes in your life. What changes would you like to see?

3

Pursuit of Peace

Increasing Your Knowledge of Who God Is and Who You Are

What is the music you are meant to hear? That with just one glance of your eyes, you can make God's heart beat faster. That He is so absolutely head over heels in love with you and me, that He is beside himself with joy. That the King of kings is utterly smitten with us...There is no greater prize than to be caught up in the ultimate romance of all the ages, realizing that you are front and center, smack dab in the absolute center of God's affections. That is the greatest song in the universe... God is not some distant, uninvolved, emotionally detached deity; rather, He is the lovesick King who longs to woo us, His heart's desire, to Himself. It says that "for the joy set before him," Jesus endured the cross (Hebrews 12:2). What is the joy that sustained Him through those darkest hours? It is "you." O that we might hear that music wafting into our soul, beckoning us to draw near. ~Introduction to the Song of Songs, *The Founders Bible*

Peace is one of the most elusive of human conditions. More and more people have been impacted by the traumatic experiences of abuse, sexual assault, violence, hurtful tongues, and the silence of family and friends. The rate of suicide is increasing. Drug abuse is a national epidemic. More and more people are struggling with anxiety and depression. Confusion and fear abound in our emotionally charged, hyper sexualized, me-driven society. In such a time and space, peace can be elusive. Is there anything the Bible can teach us about our condition? Can Jesus help us find peace?

In Genesis 4, we read about Cain and Abel, the first two children of Adam and Eve mentioned in the Bible. Both boys brought sacrifices to God, but only one was accepted. God looked with favor on Abel's offering from his flock but not on the offering of grains from his older brother, Cain. Why would God accept one offering and not the other? The story goes on.

> *Cain was very angry and dejected. Then the Lord said to Cain, "Why are you angry? Why are you dejected? If you act rightly," the Lord said, "You will be accepted. But if not, sin lies in wait at the door. Its urge is for you, yet you can rule over it"* (Genesis 4: 6-7).

God looked into Cain's heart and saw the hatred circulating through his body. God even offered Cain a chance to repent and turn away from what was about to happen. But when the two boys were together in the field, Cain rose up and killed his brother. Perhaps this is why God did not accept Cain's offering. God knew about the sin in Cain's heart even before Cain acted on it!

Then the Lord said to Cain, "Where is Abel, your brother?" And Cain said, "I do not know. Am I my brother's keeper?" God said, "What have you done? The voice of your brother's blood is crying out to Me from the ground. Now, you are cursed from the ground, which has opened its mouth to receive your brother's blood from your hand. When you cultivate the ground, it will no longer yield its strength to you" (Genesis 4: 9-12).

Instead of listening to God, Cain chose his way and had to pay the consequences. In the first book of the Bible, we learn important lessons about ourselves and God's love for us. Like Cain and Abel, each of us has the potential for good and evil in our heart. God's great love for us is manifest in His gift of free will, the freedom to choose. God could have made us love Him, but would that be true love? By definition, true love must be given freely or freely withheld.

We declare our freedom to choose, but we often fail to recognize that choices have consequences. We were created with free will but not the power to determine our own outcomes. Consequences are tied to the choices, setting up the struggle present in each of us today.

Along with free will, God also provides us with what we need to recognize bad choices and to overcome sin in our lives, if we will accept it. We spend our life learning this great truth and then choosing to act on our will or God's will. God knows what's in your heart and mine. We may not like this and we may even actively suppress this great truth. But that doesn't alter the fact that God created us with a window through which He sees what is in our heart. The other great truth that we learn right away in Genesis is that if God asks you a question, He already knows the answer!

This connection between self-awareness and God's love is also prominent in the story of the prodigal son. Here we see clearly the connection between self-awareness and peace. Most of us have heard this story often and frequently focus on one part of the story—the father's love—and for good reason. We find comfort knowing that believers are always welcomed home, as was the prodigal son. But, here is the piece that we can all identify with, having reflected on previously the story of Cain and Abel. In Luke 15:17-18, we read:

> *Coming to his senses, he (the prodigal son) thought, "How many of my father's hired workers have more than enough to eat, but here I am, dying from hunger. I shall get up and go to my father and say 'Father, I have sinned against heaven and against you.'"*

Up to this point in the story, the son was following his own dream, living according to his own will. The son's concern for his father's will, though still in his heart, was suppressed,[12] buried deep and out of mind. But, "When he came to his senses," when the son saw himself for who he truly was, then he returned home. When he saw himself as he really was and owned up to what was in his heart, he turned toward home.

No longer driven by his own will, the son acknowledged his father's will. No longer suppressed, but revealed and in plain view, the son returned home to seek forgiveness. The result? He experienced a peaceful way of life living within the will of his father.

We like to think of ourselves as good people. The world offers us many comparisons against which we can declare ourselves good. And if not good, at least, better than the Las Vegas sniper or those who are cheats and crooks on Wall Street. We all have shadows and dark places in our heart, both good and bad inclinations, positive and negative impulses that reside in our heart and mind, awaiting attention.

We've all fallen short of the mark. In the first recorded book of the Bible,[13] Job summarized our condition when he asked, "How then can man be just before a righteous God" (Job 25:4). We can try and try and try again, but at some point, the truth about our situation hits us: there is nothing we can do on our own to stand blameless in the sight of the living God.

I recognized God during a moment of great despair. I was parked on a side street one morning, not wanting to go into work, distraught by what my life had become. John Waller's song came on the radio entitled, "He Still Calls Me Son." I identified with the lyrics about a son who had come to his senses after he realized how bad his life had become. The son turned towards home and wondered if his father would ever love him again. The song climaxes when the son discovers that his father still loves him and still calls him son.

At that moment, I came to my senses and realized that I was making a mess of my life trying to do things my way. I saw myself as I truly am—a sinner. The realization and my vulnerability opened my heart to the merciful love of God. Always present but no longer suppressed by my will, the Holy Spirit flooded my heart with grace and peace. I was a sinner who needed a savior. I confessed my sinfulness and accepted God's gift, the grace of my Savior, Jesus Christ.

As we read the Bible, we understand that God sees into our hearts, knows our thoughts, and follows our every move.

Jesus, then, can accurately diagnose what ails us. In many ways, Jesus also shows us that He is the perfect remedy! When we understand who God is and who Jesus is, we know why He came and why our hearts are restless until they rest in Him.[14] "Come, come to me," Jesus says. "Come to me all you who are weary and I will give you rest" (Matthew 11:28-30).

Reading the Word of God helps us to not only learn about God but to learn more about ourselves—who we are and whose we are. The outcome? An enhanced peace of mind. Having accepted Jesus as my Lord and Savior, I began to seek God's way, not Rick's way. I now have a growing history of the peace that entered my heart and the increasing peace I began to experience in every area of my life. Though still far from perfect, the change has allowed me to modify my impact on those around me, as well.

On more than one occasion, during some tough times in my life, I have been accused of denying the reality of tough situations. People would see me navigating tough times with a sense of peace. Unable to comprehend it, they would accuse me of being in denial. As Frederick K.C. Price points out, I was not denying the reality of the tough situation; I was denying the authority of the tough situation to determine my attitude.[15] St. Paul said it best in Philippians 4:7. "And the peace of God, which surpasses all understanding will guard your heart and mind in Jesus Christ."

Our challenge is to read God's Word, and accept the love, grace, and mercy of Jesus Christ into our heart. Let's be clear. This is not a promise that we will be trouble free. As long as we live in this world, there will be trouble. But, those who get caught up in Christ can anticipate the peace that is promised to us—peace that surpasses all understanding.

Reflection

1. What areas of your life need greater peace at this time?

2. After His resurrection, Jesus commonly greeted people with a single word—Peace. How might situations in your life be changed if you were to carry with you the peace of Christ?

4

Powerful Partnership

Growing Your Image of Jesus Christ, Leveraging His Grace and Mercy

God can get tiny if we are not careful. ~Fr. Gregory Boyle

As we turn our heart to God, we learn about His peace and His power, promises, and provisions. We hear stories about how people have experienced God in their lives. In his book, *Tattoos on the Heart,* Fr. Gregory Boyle shares his life, struggles, and victories, working in the gang-ridden inner city of Los Angeles. Fr. Boyle notes that God can get tiny if we are not careful.[16] He works hard to help people increase their image of God. Perhaps you've heard the popular saying from an unknown author: "Don't tell God how big your problems are. Tell your problems how big your God is!"

Throughout the Bible, God calls people to rely on His promises and power. In the Exodus story, God warned the Israelites not to save manna from one day to the next. He was developing their reliance on Him to provide their daily bread

(Exodus 16:19). Do you remember the movie "300"? It was based on the biblical story of Gideon, as recorded in Judges 7. Gideon was called by God to fight against the Midians. He started with an army of 32,000 soldiers, but the Lord told him to whittle it down. In the end, God sent him into battle with just 300 men. How crazy is that? Was God just showing off? Maybe just a little, but God was teaching Gideon to rely on the power of the living God, not on himself and the power of his army.

My journals chronicle my own experiences with the power of God. The date was October 19, 2017. I was worried about the coming day of work. The calendar was full; the agenda items contentious. During my morning devotion, I read the story about Jesus and His disciples in a boat during a terrible storm.

> *That day when evening came, He said to his disciples, "Let us go over to the other side." Leaving the crowd behind, they took Him along, just as He was, in the boat. There were also other boats with Him. A furious squall came up, and the waves broke over the boat, so that it was nearly swamped. Jesus was in the stern, sleeping on a cushion. The disciples woke Him and said to Him, "Teacher, don't you care if we drown?" He got up, rebuked the wind and said to the waves, "Quiet! Be still!" Then the wind died down and it was completely calm. He said to his disciples, "Why are you so afraid? Do you still have no faith?" They were terrified and asked each other, "Who is this? Even the wind and the waves obey him?"* (Mark 4:35-41)

The Apostles' image of Jesus was still tiny. They had not

yet realized who Jesus was and the great power in His Word. My image of Jesus was tiny too. As we read the scriptures, we grow our image of God and our understanding of who Jesus is and the great power He possesses. As I wrapped up my devotion that morning, I asked Jesus for His peace and to help fight my battles. The day no longer looked so daunting. At bedtime that night, I reflected on how smooth the day had gone. I thanked God and peaceful sleep soon followed.

Over time, increasingly more fully caught up in Christ, I have been moved to seek the peace and power of Christ. Last year, my mom had hip surgery. This surgery was to repair muscle tissue nearly a year after the hip was replaced. Before her surgery, I organized a phone conference with my sisters to pray for Mom. I had never done this before. I was scared, not sure how my sisters or Mom would respond. God calmed my fears and gave me words to speak.

The surgery went better than expected but the real testimony to God's power came at the first follow-up appointment. The doctor was so surprised at how well Mom was doing that he ran out of the room and called for his nurse to come and see! Had I still had a tiny image of God, I would never have thought about praying over Mom. I understand that God does not always answer prayers as prayed. The lesson here is not about how prayers are answered. Instead, the lesson here is about a confidence in Christ that lead us to pray.

I remember one day when I bent over to pick up a set of keys and was unable to straighten up. I slumped to the floor. Dagmar and my friend, Ted, had to help me up. After the back spasms subsided, I struggled to the doctor's office. Along with a prescription for muscle relaxants, my doctor spoke to me like a high school football coach. "Your body can't carry all that weight!" Convicted, I started to work on my weight.

My two biggest issues were portion control and snacking throughout the day. I was able to get a handle on these issues, in large part, by reframing the changes I needed to make. I started to eat smaller portions and reducing the amount of snacks consumed as a form of spiritual fasting. My family could tell you how much I started taking smaller portions and declaring, "Just enough for flavor!" I needed the presence of the Holy Spirit to mean more to me than the larger bowl of chocolate ice cream. The power of God filled me up, and my weight began to drop. I reaped the rewards of spiritual fasting, and it wasn't even Lent!

The power of God also helped me overcome the seduction of pornography. We live in a world saturated by sex. Not too many years ago, it took effort to gain access to pornographic material. Today, it is only a click away and, in many situations, it is even forced upon us. I remember my first experience with internet pornography. It was a new drug, and I was hooked. In time, with help, I called upon the power of the Holy Spirit, and the power of God broke through my addiction. How? As I typed in porn site addresses on the computer, I would hear the Holy Spirit whisper, "My Grace is enough" (see 2 Corinthians 12:9). Feeling empowered, I was able to turn away from the computer and turn to positive input and healthy distraction until the urge passed.

After the resurrection and right before Jesus ascended into heaven, He told the apostles that "All power in heaven and on earth has been given to me" (Matthew 28:18). Do you believe this? Do you really? Are there areas in your life where you feel powerless to make a change? Perhaps you've been following a worldly prescription to achieve results, but true and lasting change has alluded you.

Believers can call upon Jesus and leverage His grace and mercy against the troubles in their lives. "For I know my plans for you," declares the Lord. "Plans to prosper you and not to harm you, plans to give you hope and a future" (Jeremiah 29:11). The result? A new source of power that is not our power but God's power washing over our lives through the ongoing ministry of Christ Jesus through the Holy Spirit.

Feeling alone in your fight? Look to the angels of God! This has been another great surprise as I have read the Bible! Consider what the writer of Hebrews says in chapter 1, verse 14: "Are not all angels ministering spirits sent to serve those who will inherit salvation?" What a comforting thought! We are not alone, and we don't have to fight our battles alone. Read God's Word and invite Christ's peace and power into your life!

J. Ligon Duncan III says, "Nobody ever encounters God and says, 'That was boring and irrelevant.' When people say that about the Bible, that says to me that they have not encountered the God of the Bible." If you haven't had such an experience, I urge you to pray for an encounter with the God of the Bible! It will change your life.

Reflection

1. How big is your God?

2. If you could change three things in your life, what would they be? How would these changes impact how you experience the world and how the world experiences you?

5

Godly Perspective
Understanding Your Place
in the Unfolding Story

My first Canadian fishing trip was with one of my three sons and a group of friends he had fished with the previous three years. I was amazed at the consistent size of the black crappie we caught. When it came time to snap some photos, I wondered if people would truly understand how big they were. Then, Erick placed his right hand next to the fish at the edge of the table. Having his hand in the picture gave it perspective that would help people truly appreciate the size of these beautiful fish.

Reading Holy Scripture and accepting Christ into our heart results in peace, power, and a godly perspective. As we seek the Lord's will, we develop a different way of looking at things that happen in our life and those things that don't happen in our life. The Bible offers us godly perspectives on every element of our life. We'll cover seven specific elements in this chapter.

- God's perspective on history
- God's perspective on your purpose
- God's perspective on free will
- God's perspective on your battle
- God's perspective on Jesus
- God's perspective on the cross
- God's perspective on forgiveness, reconciliation, and repentance
- God's perspective on history

So much of our world grooms us to get caught up in our own life and times. Reading the Bible teaches us we are also part of the unfolding story of God's creation and plan for redemption. In Genesis, we learn how everything began; and in the Book of Revelation, we learn how everything will end.

As we study God's Word, we get to know God's perspective on history, and we gain a better appreciation for our individual experience. The Apostle James asks in James 4:14, "What is your life? For you are a mist that appears for a little time and then vanishes." The Bible tells the story of paradise—paradise lost and feared gone forever, and paradise found. Though just a small part, we are all an important part of this unfolding story!

I only recently began to study Bible prophecy, but it's already been an amazing journey. I am no expert, but let me share with you one of my great surprises. At Mass, we hear prophetic Scripture at Christmas time and Easter. Isaiah, especially, expresses how God is reclaiming His creation through the virgin birth, death, resurrection, and dominion of Jesus Christ. In the weekend Scripture readings, we don't hear much about the prophecy included in the Book of

Revelation, but it is fascinating and gives us the end of the story. Since nearly a third of the Bible is prophetic, should we not engage it?

Think back to the Christmas story in the second chapter of Matthew. What three gifts did the Wise Men bring Jesus? Yes! Gold, frankincense, and myrrh. Gold for a king, frankincense for a priest, and myrrh, symbolizing how death would play a significant role in the Messiah's story. In Isaiah 60, Isaiah is prophesying about the second coming of Jesus.[17] Scripture declares that Jesus will return to earth a second time. The Bible provides us with a detailed picture about these end times and how the second coming will differ from the first coming, the virgin birth. At the second coming, Isaiah tells us, "All from Sheba shall come bearing gold and frankincense and heralding the praises of the Lord" (Isaiah 60:6).

Gifts will again play an important role, but what gift is missing at the second coming? Myrrh! When Jesus comes a second time, there will be no more death! Jesus is our Savior, alive now and forever! The Bible has hundreds of prophecies about the first coming of the Messiah, and there is evidence to conclude they all came true in the person of Jesus of Nazareth. Should we question the prophecies about the second coming of Christ?

God's Perspective on Our Purpose

As we learn more about the unfolding story, we learn that God has a plan for each of us. But if our life is but a mist, is there any real purpose to it? Is our life just what we can make of it while we're here, or is there some larger purpose? Each of us has been knitted together with talents, gifts, and experiences that make us a unique ambassador to a given place and time.

Think about a football game. The quarterback throws a pass, and it is caught by a member of his team. Then he throws a pass that is caught by a member of the opposing team. They are both catches. What makes one good and the other bad? The one catch helps your team; the other one hurts it. You have to know the purpose of the game to know what is truly good and bad. The same is true for us. We need to know God's perspective on the purpose of our life.

The summation of the Bible tells us our purpose is to know God and make God known. We all have a specific occupation and calling, but God also has a specific purpose for each of us as it relates to the unfolding story. Even in our short time on this earth, God declares His purpose for each of us. We can look at specific people and easily see the purpose of God. The life of the late Billy Graham was known to nearly everyone and God's purpose for him easily identified.

But, for others, perhaps you, it can be hard to discern any specific purpose. We experience times of struggle and pain and disappointment, when it can be really hard to see any divine purpose. Do you think God has a purpose for your life? Will God help you along the path if you're on the path God laid out for you? The Bible tells us that God, indeed, has a plan for you! As Rick Warren declares; "There might be accidental parents, but there are no accidental children."[18] You matter! We are created in the image and likeness of God. If you ever find yourself questioning your value, get caught up in Christ and pray to better understand your purpose.

God's Perspective on Free Will

Our life is a series of decisions. We either make them assertively with purpose or we decline to act and, instead, passively defer to other forces and voices in our environment. We have freedom to choose. God loves us and desires a relationship with us. Could God have made us love Him? Certainly, but that would not be love. Love, by definition, is freely given. Even the Genie couldn't make Jasmine fall in love with Aladdin!

The free will that we are blessed with attests to the greatness of God's love. As we saw with Cain and Abel, having free will also sets us up with a mighty struggle. As I learned more about God and His plans, purposes, and provisions, I began to pray for more direction in my life, which helped me see more clearly the different choices I have each day.

So much is made of freedom these days and exercising free will. It's great, but the Bible communicates an important truth here. We get to determine our own choices, but we don't get to determine our own outcomes. If we misuse and abuse illicit drugs, we'll have to wrestle with the consequences of addiction. If our key relationships are riddled with fruitless arguments and mistrust, and if we seek only the satisfaction of our needs rather than serving others, we should expect to face hard times and the likely end of the relationship. Reading God's Word gives us a clear direction for our lives and sets up the choices we have between God's way and our way.

One of my favorite stories from the Old Testament is about Elijah and his contest with the Baal gods on Mount Carmel. Here is the scene: Solomon, King David's son, has passed away. The nation of Israel has passed from the glorious days of Solomon's reign to a period of division. Many are walking away from their faith and worshipping false gods. There is a great gathering of Israelites along with 450 prophets of Baal at Mount Carmel. Elijah asks all those present: "How long will you straddle the issue? If the Lord is God, follow him. If Baal, follow him" (1 Kings 18: 21).

Receiving no answer from the people, Elijah sets up a contest. Elijah proposed that two oxen be brought forward. The Baal prophets would choose one, and Elijah would get the other. Both would cut up their ox and place it on wood but add no fire. The Baal prophets would call on their god, and Elijah would call on the Lord. Whichever God answers with fire, He is God. Everyone agreed to the terms of the contest.

The prophets of Baal were the first to go. They called out from morning until noon with no response. Elijah taunted them, "Call louder, for he is a god; either he is busy doing business or may be on a journey; perhaps he is asleep and needs to be awakened. So, they called out louder and slashed themselves according to their ritual until blood gushed over them" (1 Kings 18:27-28). Evening came and still no response.

Elijah then called everyone closer to him. In order to win an unmistakable victory for God, Elijah built up an altar with 12 stones (signifying the 12 tribes of Israel) and placed the ox on top of it. He also had a deep trench dug around the altar. He told servants to pour water over the ox not one, not two, but three times. The water filled up the trench.

When the time of the evening sacrifice had come, Elijah prayed, "O Lord, the God of Abraham, Isaac, and Israel (Jacob), today let it be known that You are God in Israel and that I am Your servant and I have done all these things at Your command. Answer me, O Lord, answer me, that this people may know that You, O Lord, are God, and that You have turned their hearts back to you" (1 Kings 18:36-37).

When all eyes were fixed on the altar, God answered! "The Lord's fire came down and devoured the burnt offering, wood, stones, and dust, and lapped up the water in the trench" (1 Kings 18:38). The people fell to the ground and worshipped the Lord.

The point of the story remains the same: faith has always been a free-market concept. We get to choose to whom we will pledge our allegiance: the Lord or some other god. God loves us, but God won't force us to love Him. Love, by definition, is freely given and freely withheld. But we need to keep in mind that if we choose not to follow God, God will give us over to our own desires (Romans 1:24). Put another way, we will say to God, "Thy will be done," or God will say to us, "Thy will be done."

I liken this to parents who allow their children to experience consequences of their actions to learn important lessons. Can you see situations in your life when God might be doing the same thing? And, just as parents remain vigilant and ready to embrace their children as the lesson is learned, God waits for us to recognize His loving ways and return home! We are today's prodigal children always being invited home.

God's Perspective on Our Battle

With free will, comes tension. We've all had days when life feels like a battle. We have days that feel like a battle because they are one! St. Paul encourages us to put on the armor of God. Why else would we need armor if we're not in a battle? We are encouraged to put on the belt of truth, the breastplate of righteousness, the shoes of the gospel, and the helmet of salvation. We are also told to pick up the sword of the spirit and the shield of faith (Ephesians 6:11-17). This is our everyday armor.

Reading the Bible gives us a more complete perspective on this battle and who's involved. Let's play a little game to learn a huge lesson. I'll say a word, and you think of its opposite. Up—down; right—wrong; tall—short; God—Satan? Like many people, I used to think that Satan was the opposite of God. Satan is not the opposite of God. He's more like the opposite of the Archangel Michael. Let me explain.

Lucifer, who would become the one we know as Satan, was an angel created by God. The Bible tells us that Lucifer was high-ranking and powerful (Ezekiel 28:11-19, and Isaiah 14: 12-17). But he was also an angel who exercised his free will and wanted to be like God. Think back to the story of Adam and Eve in the garden. What was the original sin? God said they could eat of any tree except the tree in the center of the garden, the tree of knowledge of good and evil. When we think we can somehow determine right from wrong, we make ourselves Godlike. Lucifer wanted to be God and committed this original sin. Dr. David Jeremiah explains that the Bible teaches us that God, because of His holy and perfect nature, cannot abide in or be in the presence of sin.[19] Because Lucifer committed the first sin by wanting to become like God, he was kicked out of heaven.

Satan is not on an equal level with God! The devil still answers to God; and we know that, one day, at the appointed time, God will take back the earth from this prince of darkness! (Revelation 20: 7-10) This may be the best news of the day! But we must never doubt the power of darkness. Satan tricked Eve into biting the apple and then Adam did too. That original sin changed things for all of us. Our battle is real, but we won't win unless we recognize what and whom we are up against. I know I have nothing of myself that I can bring against Satan. I praise God that I have within reach, the one power that is above all power—the name of Jesus Christ.

God's Perspective on Jesus

When we think of Jesus, we always need to keep in mind His two natures—He was fully human and fully divine. As fully human, He had the same free will that we have. Jesus was free to make decisions between good and bad, just as we do; to pursue His will, or God the Father's will; seeking to be God or letting God be God. As we just saw, Satan considered equality with God something to be grasped. Did Jesus? In Philippians 2:6 we read: "Let this mind be in you which was also in Christ Jesus: Who, existing in the form of God, did not consider equality with God something to be grasped, but emptied Himself, taking the form of a servant."

Jesus did not seek to be equal with God. His entire life was dedicated to doing His Father's will. In doing so, Jesus faced all the temptations, pains, and trials that we face in our own lives. This helps us have a deeper appreciation for this verse from Hebrews.

Therefore, since we have such a great high priest who has passed through the heavens, Jesus the Son of God, let us hold firmly to what we profess. For we do not have a high priest who is unable to sympathize with our weaknesses, but we have one who was tempted in every way that we are, yet, was without sin. Let us then approach the throne of grace with confidence, so that we may receive mercy and find grace to help us in our time of need (Hebrews 4:15).

When we are tempted to think of Jesus as simply divine, we need to keep in mind that Jesus was just as human as we are. However, He made different choices than we often do. Jesus dedicated His life to God's will and His disciplined life took Him all the way to Calvary. The cross of Christ takes center stage in our churches. What makes the cross so important?

God's Perspective on the Cross

Jesus hung on the cross for nearly three hours. Jesus, in His full humanity, then called out to God, "Eli, Eli, lema sabachthani?" "My God, My God, why have you forsaken Me?" (Matthew 27:46). Had God forsaken Jesus? Think back to the story of Lucifer. God cannot abide with or live in the presence of sin. Because of his sinfulness, Lucifer could no longer reside in the presence of God. Jesus experienced abandonment because of the sin He was carrying. But Jesus was without sin. So, whose sins was he carrying? Mine and yours.

At that moment, the curtain of the temple was torn in two from top to bottom. The earth shook, the rocks split, and the tombs broke open. The bodies of many Holy people who had died were raised to life (Matthew 27:51).

Jesus accomplished two critical things that day on the cross. First, He answered the question first raised by Job: How can mortal man stand before a righteous God? The answer is only if we are covered by the blood of Jesus Christ. God is a just God and that means that poor choices have outcomes, and the charges need to be covered. Cursed by the original sin of Adam, we have all sinned and fall short of the glory of God (Romans 3:23). Someone needs to pay for our poor choices, our sins. This is where we begin to understand the boundless love of God. In creating us in His image, God longs to be in a loving relationship with each of us, both now and for all of eternity. Enter Jesus Christ: "For God so loved the world that He sent His only Son, that whosoever believes in him should not perish, but, have everlasting life" (John 3:16).

With sins forgiven, believers are free to engage life with peace, power, and perspective. Yet, as you know, this doesn't somehow save us from the trials of life. In fact, the Bible testifies to the fact that life on this earth is hard. This brings us to the second great outcome of the crucifixion. In dying on the cross, Jesus, the second person of the Holy Trinity, made way for the third person of the Holy Trinity, the Holy Spirit. Through the power of God, the Holy Spirit carries on the ministry of Jesus Christ. Read Scripture and see how Jesus loved people, was angry with sinners, and gave hope to believers. Place yourself in the gospel stories and invite the Holy Spirit to love you, discipline you, and save you!

Before we leave the cross, I want to share with you one more way that I have been surprised by study. The Bible tells us that the guards broke the legs of the other two criminals crucified along with Jesus. I never had a full appreciation for what this signifies until I read Lee Strobel's book, *The Case for Christ.*[20]

The book explains why the guards broke their legs. In

short, by breaking their legs, people who were crucified would be dead in seconds from asphyxiation. It's important to know this because when the guards came to Jesus, they saw that He was already dead. If He wasn't, they would have broken His legs too to kill Him.

Can we know this confidently? In addition to the history recorded in the Bible, there is also recorded history from non-Christian sources that document the crucifixion and resurrection of Jesus. Titus Flavius Josephus was one of the earliest Jewish historians. He lived during the time of Jesus and the early years of the Way, which would become what we know as Christianity. Josephus documented the same events recorded in the Bible including the crucifixion and reports of the resurrection. In fact, there are many historians and public figures whose personal writings chronical these pivotal historical events. Some of these writers include Pliny the Younger, Cornelius Tacitus, Celsus, and Tacitus.[21]

There is one more line of evidence from the scriptures themselves. When people point to differences between the four gospels and claim they can't be reliable, others embrace the differences as evidence of their validity. Author J. Warner Wallace was an L.A. County homicide detective when he decided to apply his investigative skills to prove that the Gospels were unreliable. In the end, as so many do, he discovered that the Gospel testimonies complimented each other and validated the story of Jesus, including His resurrection. Wallace walks you through his investigation and his findings in his book, *Cold-Case Christianity*.

It's important for us to know confidently that Christ died on the cross at Calvary. Evidence shows us that the Romans were good at what they did. No one survived crucifixion.

The point is that Jesus was crucified and died on the cross. Dead. End of story. But, thanks be to God, it wasn't the end of His story!

A believer's great joy comes from a confident belief in the glory and triumph of the resurrection. Even the 19th century, world-renowned historian and professor at the distinguished Oxford University, Dr. Thomas Arnold wrote publicly that "I know of no one fact in the history of mankind which is proved by better and fuller evidence of every sort...than the resurrection of Jesus Christ."[22]

God's Perspective on Forgiveness, Reconciliation, and Repentance

The heart of our faith is a real and life-changing relationship with God through His Son, Jesus Christ. As with all our meaningful relationships, our heart is deeply involved. When we turn away from the brokenness of our heart, we turn toward the loving and sacred heart of Jesus. This is where we grasp the impact of sin in our lives. As we learned earlier, God cannot abide in the presence of sin. If we want God to abide in us and live in our heart, we need to confess our sin. We need to repent and be forgiven. Throughout the Bible, we see God's tender mercy, long-suffering, and His willingness to forgive a contrite heart. By His willingness to go to the cross, Jesus secured this gift for all who confess His name and invite Him into their heart.

Think back to a time when you asked for and received forgiveness from a loved one or friend. Do you remember how it felt to be restored to that relationship? Imagine what it feels like to be restored to your relationship with the Creator of the Universe!

Sin and forgiveness of sin are a primary focus of our Lord's ministry. The reality of sin and the truth about our need for forgiveness can be challenging topics. They challenged people in Jesus' day too. Consider the following account from Luke's Gospel.

One day as Jesus was teaching, Pharisees and teachers of the law were sitting there who had come from every village of Galilee and Judea and Jerusalem, and the power of the Lord was with Him for healing. And some men brought on a stretcher a man who was paralyzed; they were trying to bring him in and set him in His presence. But not finding a way to bring him in because of the crowd, they went up on the roof and lowered him on the stretcher through the tiles into the middle in front of Jesus. When He saw their faith, He said, "As for you, your sins are forgiven." Then the scribes and Pharisees began to ask themselves, "Who is this who speaks blasphemies? Who but God alone can forgive sins?" Jesus knew their thoughts and said to them in reply, "What are you thinking in your hearts? Which is easier, to say, 'Your sins are forgiven,' or to say, 'Rise and walk?' But that you may know that the Son of Man has authority on earth to forgive sins'—He said to the man who was paralyzed, 'I say to you, rise, pick up your stretcher, and go home.'" He stood up immediately before them, picked up what he had been lying on, and went home, glorifying God. Then astonishment seized them all and they glorified God, and, struck with awe, they said, "We have seen incredible things today" (Luke 5:17-26).

Acts of forgiveness and reconciliation are powerful experiences. Our physical and emotional brokenness do not break down our relationship with God. Sin does. There is no question why the Sacrament of Reconciliation is a formative experience in the Catholic Church.

We confess our sins to restore our relationship with God. There is a second reason to confess our sins. Scripture illuminates this truth that can provide us a new perspective on our battles. In Matthew 18:21-35, Jesus tells us the story about forgiveness and how unconfessed sin can impact our life. There was a master who forgave a servant a great debt. But then the servant refused to forgive a man who owed him a much smaller sum of money. The servant was discovered and sent back to the master: "You wicked servant," the Master said. "I forgave you your entire debt because you begged me to. Should you not have had pity on your fellow servant, as I had pity on you?"

Now, watch this:

> *Then in anger, his master handed him over to the torturers until he should pay back the whole debt. Jesus went on to say, "So will my heavenly father do to you, unless each of you forgive his brother from his heart."*

Think about the struggles in your life: persistent and negative patterns of behavior that you have been unable to change; life situations that seem stuck and unmovable; troubling relationships that seem to go on and on. Is it possible that they could be connected to unconfessed sin? Think of the Lord's Prayer: "Forgive us our trespasses as we forgive those who trespass against us."

There is an important lesson here for all of us. By acknowledging and accepting the truth about our situations, we become more aware of the grace and mercy we experience in Christ. Our relationship with Christ empowers us to take ownership of our thoughts, words, and deeds. Taking ownership of the whole of our lives, we seek forgiveness from those around us and, most of all, forgiveness from God. We will uncover wounds and brokenness that may surprise us. In getting caught up in Christ, we grow in our understanding over time and how God provides for our healing and deliverance.

It would be negligent if we were to move on without recognizing that the whole of our experiences also include times when we have been wronged by others. Returning to our first aid metaphor, they might be paper cuts, broken bones, or the full loss of life. These events might be connected to deeply emotional and life-changing experiences for some of you.

It is important to recognize the clear difference between forgiveness and reconciliation. With support and help from the Holy Spirit, we may forgive a wrong done to us, but we may not be ready or even interested in reconciliation with the person(s). Having said that, we could point to people who have moved through forgiveness to reconciliation after incredible pain. With God, nothing is impossible. But that is often a separate decision that is best thought out and prayed over with trusted advisors. Our willingness to forgive is not just about the person who hurt us, but even more about our recognition of what God offers us and the other person(s) through the blood of Jesus Christ.

Sometimes our pain leads us to thoughts of and desires for revenge. I have known this too. Again, at the risk of making too little of what can be a weighty matter, keep in mind what Paul urged believers to do in Romans 12:19: "Beloved, do not look for revenge but leave room for the wrath; for it is written 'Vengeance is mine, I will repay, says the Lord.'" Make no mistake, there are times when this is easier said than done. However, as we pursue a relationship with God and aim to follow the teaching of Jesus, we seek this mindset just the same.

This book is about maintaining and prioritizing our relationship with God. As we grow in our faith and seek a closer walk with Christ, we must pray daily that God will reveal any unconfessed sins so that we can bring them into the light of confession, seek forgiveness, and ask to be released from those things causing us stress and pain. This, in turn, helps us repent of poor choices. Repentance is about replacing negative and unhealthy patterns of thought and behavior with those that line us up with the will of God for our life.

This can be easier said than done. You might be facing patterns that have been present in your life for decades. Are you having doubts about making certain changes in your life? If you're like me, you might be thinking there is no way to get beyond your pattern of troublesome behavior or overcoming the ongoing temptation of drug use, pornography, greed, whatever it might be for you. Here is great encouragement.

No trial has come to you but what is human. God is faithful and will not let you be tried beyond your strength; but with the trial he will also provide a way out, so that you may be able to bear it (1 Corinthians 10:13).

Count on this truth. The next time you are tempted, look for the way out! It's there. God has promised that it will be there!

Here is a metaphor that I hope will help us capture fully the benefit of having a godly perspective. In the skies overhead, airline pilots are in communication with air-traffic controllers. The pilots count on them to know the final destination of the aircraft but also to know about any obstacles that lie in its path.

There are times when the dangers are such that pilots are directed to change flight paths. How much sense would it make for pilots to second-guess these directions or even turn off the radio all together? The input that controllers provide to pilots is not criticism but points of correction. They have a perspective that the pilots do not have access to. God has a perspective that we do not have access to. Reading Holy Scripture provides us God's perspective by which we can adjust our flight plan and make in-flight corrections, when needed.

Reflection

1 How might a godly perspective change your understanding of an event in your life or a decision you are facing?

2. In what areas of your life do you need to modify your "flight path" or change your destination?

6

Pure Thoughts

Avoiding the Consequences of Bad Thinking

A young man walked into my office one day carrying Jerry Coyne's book *Why Evolution Is True*. He shared with me all he was learning about the first proteins and other building blocks that multiplied to give us living organisms. I asked him where those first elements came from. He sat quietly, unable to give an answer. We talked briefly about the difference between understanding the operation of life and the origination of life. We compared the different accounts for the beginning of our universe and the genesis of life on earth, including the creation account. He raised his left hand, examined it at length, and then pondered out loud, "I have always wondered...if we really evolved, why did we evolve like this?"

In getting caught up in Christ, believers enjoy the results of peace, power, and having a godly perspective, but let's be real. All of this puts us at odds with the world. We live in an age when the world is busy trying to deny God and to eliminate all things related to Jesus and religious freedom, in general. Scientists claim to have everything figured out and, if we give them time, they will show proof that the universe and all we know about life came into being and will proceed onward without divine intervention. Philosophers want us to believe that truth is relative, and that there is no right or wrong but just what you and I think is right and wrong, true and false.

People want to do their own thing, but we get angry when a man sticks a long gun out a hotel window and mows down country music fans or when a kid takes guns to school and shoots up his classmates and teachers. If people want to do their own thing, doesn't this mean everyone gets the right to do their own thing? If there is no standard for what is good, how can anything be bad?

Viktor Frankl was a Jewish psychiatrist and survivor of the concentration camps of World War II. After life in a Nazi death camp, he summarized his experience with truth, of what is good and bad.

> If we present man with a concept of man which is not true, we may well corrupt him. When we present him as an automation of reflexes, as a mind-machine, as a bundle of instincts, as a pawn of drives and reactions, as a mere product of instincts, heredity, and environment, we feed the despair to which man is, in any case, already prone. I became acquainted with the last stages of corruption in my second concentration camp in Auschwitz. The gas chambers of Auschwitz were the ultimate consequence of the theory that man is nothing but the product of heredity and environment, or as the Nazis like to say, "of blood and soil." I am absolutely convinced that the gas chambers...were ul-

timately prepared not in some ministry or other in Berlin, but rather at the desks and in the lecture halls of nihilistic scientists and philosophers.[23]

As a believer, I am convinced truth does exist. A moral standard exists for good and bad, right and wrong. Whether we embrace this truth or suppress it makes an unmistakable difference in our lives. Is it important for us to know how to distinguish good from bad, pleasing from displeasing, perfect from imperfect? It involves effort to consider the impact of our choices on our life and on the life of those around us.

Increasingly, the world is convinced that people can determine and choose their own truth about what is good and bad, right and wrong. To what extent is this happening with you today? While we stand up for Christ, there are others who are standing up for Satan and devil worship. For example, students have now organized satanic students at NC State, in part, to "reject tyrannical authority" (N.C. State).[24] And, just so you don't run out of things to think about, The Satanic Temple is now bringing After School Satan Clubs to public schools near you (After School Satan).[25] Could there be a more drastic difference between good and evil?

Does reading God's Word enhance our awareness of truth and avoid the outcomes of negative thinking? St. Paul declared the answer clearly in Romans 12:1-2.

> *I urge you therefore, brothers, by the mercies of God, to offer your bodies as a living sacrifice, holy and pleasing to God, your spiritual worship. Do not conform yourselves to the age but be transformed by the renewal of your mind, that you may discern what is the will of God, what is good and pleasing and perfect.*

Hebrews 2:1 says, "For this reason you must pay closer attention to what we have heard so that you do not drift away." This has been a challenge for believers throughout history. It's that free will thing again that calls into question what frequency we will tune to on our mental radios, which voice will we listen to: God or humankind? The Creator or the created?

Jesus made an astounding claim when He said, "I am the way, the truth, and the life" (John 14:6). This played out in a notable court room drama! During his trial, Jesus was questioned by Pontius Pilate. Jesus answered, "For this reason I was born and have come into the world, to testify to the truth. Everyone who belongs to the truth listens to My voice." Pilate then asked the right question: "What is truth?" And, having said this, he went out again to the Jews (John 18: 37). While Pilate asked the right question, he didn't stick around for the answer. Either Jesus is the way and the truth and the life, or He isn't. There is no middle ground. Will we stick around for the answer?

We can search the Word for understanding and guidance in making decisions about all the important things in our life. The Bible declares God's perspective on life and death, pain and suffering, diversity and race relations, our personal relationships, parenting, economics, and even government. Did you know that the Bible was the number one source of input for the founding documents of the United States Declaration of Independence and the Constitution?[26] The founding era certainly had controversies and dark moments. Nevertheless, the documents remain unique.

The world will also share its opinions on the same subjects. Talk with others; observe the outcomes of different schools of thought; study history for a better understanding of how different worldviews have played out on the world stage. You will quickly see the differences. We can judge a tree by its fruits. Then, once again, we are left with the choice: Will we pursue God's way or our way?

If we are not careful and vigilant, we can be deceived. Do you remember the Pandora affect? Deception often leads to bad thinking. Studying the Word helps us enhance our good thinking, but we also need to be cautious as we read. One of the ways that I found myself deceived was by taking verses out of context and failing to grasp the full meaning of godly messages. If we don't know the full story or the context, we are at risk of being deceived by getting only half the message. A few examples will help make the point.

> *If any of you lacks wisdom, he should ask God, who gives generously to all without finding fault, and it will be given to him* (James 1:5).

This sounds great but watch the next verse:

> *But he must ask in faith, without doubting, because he who doubts is like a wave of the sea, blown and tossed by the wind. That man should not expect to receive anything from the Lord. He is a double-minded man, unstable in all his ways* (James 1:6).

Does verse 6 modify the full meaning of verse 5?

"God makes all things beautiful" (Ecclesiastes 3:11) is a wonderful sentiment but one that we can struggle to accept, given our experiences and observations of the world around us, until we read the rest of the verse: "God makes all things beautiful IN HIS TIME." That is a very different message and one that we can, regardless of our experiences and even more so during tough times, hold onto with both hands as we hope in our Lord and Savior, Jesus Christ, and seek wisdom in a godly perspective.

"Do not judge, or you too will be judged" (Matthew 7:1). The world highjacks this verse and declares that even the Bible says not to judge. But is that what it says? Read the next verses.

> *For in the same way you judge others, you will be judged, and with the measure you use, it will be measured to you. Why do you look at the speck of sawdust in your brother's eye and pay no attention to the plank in your own eye? How can you say to your brother, 'let me take the speck out of your eye,' when all the time there is a plank in your own eye? You hypocrite, first take the plank out of your eye, and then you will see clearly to remove the speck from your brother's eye* (Matthew 7:2-5)

When we read the rest of the message, the Bible actually tells us how to judge. This starts with us getting our own act together and takes us back to the importance of self-knowledge, of us understanding who we are, and coming to our senses, as did the prodigal son. Reading the Bible helps us understand the full and true teachings of Jesus. This requires a commitment to study it for the full message, not simply feed on feel-good verses that we can highjack for our own purposes.

I discovered this dynamic as it relates to the entire Bible. Reading the Old Testament and the Book of Revelation brought clarity to my study of the New Testament. In reading the New Testament only, it's like watching the second act of a play and trying to understand its full meaning without seeing the first act and the last scene. As we develop an understanding of the Bible as the Word of God and as we accept Jesus' statement about being the Way, the Truth, and the Life, we can enhance our awareness of truth and help avoid the outcomes of bad thinking.

Reflection

1. Reflect on situations in your life where you feel you may have been deceived about the truth of the situation or neglected to consider the truth about the situation.

2. Recall decisions you've made in your life that you now understand were the result of misinformation or bad thinking. What have you learned from those situations?

7

Persuaded and Persuasive

Unraveling the dynamic of
Receiving, Sharing, and Witnessing

Anita Dittman was a young Jewish girl. As Adolph
Hitler began his rise to power, she was introduced to
Jesus Christ. Running away from Nazi work camps
and enduring illness and injury, she was persuaded of
the faithfulness of the Messiah. She gave her life to
Christ and shared her faith with others in the camps.
One day she saw a woman curled up in a corner
crying. It was a German nurse who had tried to kill
Anita. Anita felt God had brought her to the nurse to
comfort her. Anita argued with God, telling God all
the evil things the nurse had done to her. "Then I
thought to myself how stupid. God already knew all of
that." Anita closed her eyes to pray. "I saw in my
minds eye Christ hanging on the cross saying 'Father,
forgive them.' I asked God to forgive me for my terrible attitude. Take the bitterness out of my heart and
put in your love and then I will be able to do it." Anita
sat down beside the nurse. As she sobbed, the nurse
told Anita that she had been raped many times. Anita

sobbed with her. Then, the nurse recognized Anita and pushed herself away. "How can you comfort me? I tried to kill you." Anita responded, "I know, but with Christ's help, I forgive you." ~Anita Dittman, *Trapped in Hitler's Hell*

If peace and power, a godly perspective, and pure thoughts yield such a great harvest, why are so many walking away from the faith? Why are our churches so empty on Sunday? Why did it take me nearly 40 years to arrive at this point in my faith? I had so many questions and doubts along the way. Dr. David Jeremiah points out that all of us, at times, have doubts and are even ashamed of the gospel. He has found that the reasons usually fall into one of four categories: intellectual reasons, philosophical reasons, social reasons, and moral reasons.[27]

Working professionally in higher education for nearly 25 years, I was constantly exposed to arguments against the existence of God. I've also been told that the Jesus story is just a story made up for people who can't handle reality. Perhaps you've heard people say that the gospels aren't the same so they can't be true and the moral teachings are so outdated Christianity has no value. One Sunday night at the dinner table, our family got into a conversation about what the children were learning at school. I said something about God, and one of the kids asked me the question that stopped me cold. "But, Papa, how do you know God is real?" I had no answer.

This moment propelled me into a focused search for answers. For a time, I became a member of the book-a-month club. I was up early reading and then reading again before bed. I was no longer listening to music while I worked out. I was listening to Bible teaching. Jesus taught that blessed are they who hunger and thirst for righteousness for they will be satisfied (Matthew 5:6). I was being filled up and satisfied by the Word of God.

Months later, I had the opportunity to speak with a young man. He was open about the struggles he was having with mental health issues and a number of suicide attempts. He made a comment that gave me the chance to ask him if he believed in God. "No," he said. "I am an agnostic. I don't believe in things that are not real." He gave himself lots of credit for being well-read. He was planning to major in philosophy at college. I connected with him and responded with a question. "I totally agree with you. I only believe in things that are true too. What do you make of the historical documents from secular sources that provide evidence that Jesus of Nazareth was a real man?" He wasn't sure how to answer the question.

In his book, *Tactics*, Gregory Koukl explains his simple approach when talking with people about God. His goal is to ask a question that they must find an answer to, so he could put a pebble in their shoe.[28] In time, as we learn answers to our questions, we feel confident to share our faith. In sharing our faith, we become witnesses to the difference Jesus makes in our life and in the world. The Lord can then utilize this witness to reach other believers and non-believers, person to person, faith to faith. The apostle Paul testified to this dynamic in his life.

> *For I am not ashamed of the gospel, for it is the power of God for the salvation to everyone who believes, to the Jew*

first, and also to the Greek. For in it the righteousness of
God is revealed from faith to faith (Romans 1:16-17).

As we get caught up in Christ, our mind is renewed. Our reshaped mind results in different decisions that alter the way we experience life and the way others experience us. In time, people will experience you as being different from others and maybe even different from the person you used to be. Some will ask you for an explanation.

In 1 Peter 3:15, we are instructed, "In your hearts revere Christ as Lord. Always be prepared to give an answer to everyone who asks you to give the reason for the hope that is in you." As we live our life, we will have the opportunity to answer questions and offer godly perspectives. In doing so, we persuasively share the Good News!

Nervous? I was full of fear at the thought that Jesus might ask me to speak on His behalf. Many Catholics get nervous at the simple mention of the E-word: evangelization. You can take comfort knowing that something will happen in you as Christ works through you.

In Romans chapter 8:38, Paul addresses how this dynamic impacted his life. As he was speaking about his belief that nothing was more powerful than the love of God in Christ Jesus, he said, "I am persuaded." Martyn Loyd-Jones explains the importance of this statement.

> He (Paul) is not saying all this simply because he happens to have a particular feeling in him at the moment. Neither is he just hoping-hoping against hope. What he says is, "I am certain." It is interesting to note that he puts this in the passive (tense), "I am persuaded," which means "I have come, through a

process of persuasion, to a settled conclusion." That is the true content of the phrase. He does not persuade himself; something else has persuaded him. He is passive. The result is that, as the result of the process of persuasion, he has come to the settled conclusion; he is certain. It is an absolute certainty, beyond any doubt whatsoever.[29]

Before we ever become persuasive, we will be persuaded by the love of God, overshadowed by the power of the Holy Spirit.

Over the years, I have worn many a t-shirt for work events and at events where I was volunteering. You may know the type of shirts I am talking about. On the back is always something like "Volunteer" or "STAFF" or "Event Staff." Something happens to our perspective when we are wearing these shirts. We are suddenly tuned into anyone who calls for help or asks a question. The person may be totally out of sight, but we hear the "Excuse me! Can you help?" At those times, we are no longer driven by our wants and needs, our plans and turmoil. We are representing the team or the organization.

Much the same takes place after Jesus enters our heart and we put on Christ. We become tuned into our world in a new way. We continue to take care of our business, to struggle through our own stuff, but we also answer the calls for help. To some degree, different for all of us according to our spiritual gifts, we become persuasive in our service to the Kingdom. This takes place after we are brought to the same conclusion that St. Paul reached on the truth about Jesus Christ—absolute certainty, beyond any doubt, whatsoever.

Only heaven will reveal how people have come to know Jesus, but if God chooses to use you in some way, don't worry about your deficiencies, troubles, and dark spaces. As someone once said, God can draw straight lines with crooked sticks!

Reflection

1. On a scale of 1 to 10, how certain are you of the truth about Jesus Christ?

2. How do you currently feel about the notion that God might ask you to be a persuasive voice in the ears of someone in your sphere of influence?

8

The Path Forward
Moving Ahead Without All the Answers

Picture yourself holding on to one end of a spiritual bungee cord. What you anchor the other end of the bungee cord to will have a profound impact on how you experience the world and how the world experiences you. When we anchor the other end of the bungee cord to Christ, the Holy Spirit will pull us closer to Christ. Even when we pull away from God, the Holy Spirit will pull us back to God. If we try to move toward God while the other end of our bungee cord is still connected to a different anchor, eventually the strength of the cord will pull us back to that anchor. When we give our lives to Christ, we anchor our lives to His Word. Moving our anchor from an existing point to Christ is a leap of faith. There is often a period of uncertainty and vulnerability that follows the surrender. Fear not!

Getting caught up in Christ has changed my life. Full disclosure? This all took me by surprise. After all, I was raised in a good Catholic home and survived 12 years of Catholic education. I added four more years at a Christian college. It wasn't until I entered the fourth decade of my life that I began to understand what was really taking place. I was moving from belief that Jesus is the son of God to believing in Jesus as my personal Lord and Savior.

The Gospels proclaim that even the evil spirits knew that Jesus was the son of God but they didn't believe in him.

They went to Capernaum, and when the Sabbath came, Jesus went into the synagogue and began to teach. The people were amazed at his teaching, because he taught them as one who had authority, not as the teachers of the law. Just then a man in their synagogue who was possessed by an impure spirit cried out, "What do you want with us, Jesus of Nazareth? Have you come to destroy us? I know who you are—the Holy One of God!"

"Be quiet!" said Jesus sternly. "Come out of him!" The impure spirit shook the man violently and came out of him with a shriek. The people were all so amazed that they asked each other, "What is this? A new teaching—and with authority! He even gives orders to impure spirits and they obey him." News about him spread quickly over the whole region of Galilee (Mark 1: 21-24).

There is a big difference between knowing a truth and being persuaded by it.

To know a Bible truth, you have only to read it: to be persuaded of it in the Lord Jesus involved the fact, first, that the truth in question touches your own personal safety before God; and, second, that your heart has so been enlightened by the Holy Spirit, and your will so won over-'persuaded'-that confidence, heart-satisfied persuasion results.[30]

We return, a final time, to our choice: God's way or our way? Once persuaded, the latter option goes away. We find ourselves committed to God's way. Read God's Word and pray to be persuaded. Don't settle for the world's version of peace or even what you think you can achieve on your own. Get caught up in Christ. Don't count on your own abilities or power to achieve goals or make changes in your life. Get caught up in Christ.

Don't buy into the world's perspective on who you are, what your purpose is, or who your enemy is. Get caught up in Christ. Don't subscribe to your own way of thinking or the contaminated thinking of the world. Get caught up in Christ. Don't put limits on what God can do in you, for you, and through you to persuade those around you about the truth of biblical Christianity. Get caught up in Christ.

Please know that we often move forward without having all the answers. You will likely have lots of questions and perhaps lingering doubts. Let that be okay. Start by going to God in prayer, acknowledge that you have sinned, and ask Jesus Christ to come into your heart. The power of the Holy Spirit will lead you from there. How people read the Bible and pursue Christ will look differently for each of us. However, there are some good starting blocks from which we can all begin. Start small and make up a plan that works for you.

There are great daily devotionals that include a short Bible verse and application for the day. Read the Gospel of

John, one chapter a day. If you are really short on time, read the Gospel of Mark—it's the shortest! As you come across verses that speak to you in a special way, write them down in a journal and memorize them. How important is it to memorize Scripture? Look to Jesus for the answer. How did Jesus respond to the devil's temptations in the desert? He quoted Old Testament scripture! (Matthew 4:1-11)

Connect with a vibrant church community and consider joining a Bible study group. If your locale does not offer you such a community, you may find safe harbor with communities on the web or through social media. In these situations, the Word of God and other pertinent literary resources will be of greater value.

I just promoted resources made possible by modern technology. Yet, this same technology has contributed an immense amount of clamor and confusion. In our noisy worlds, I also believe it will be critical for you to spend time daily in the "classroom of silence."[31] Matthew Kelly describes this as a time each day when we shut off the noise and distraction of the world and tune directly into God. Yes, we will hear God speak to us!

If currently attending church, ask your church leaders to support the "Take your Bible to Mass" program. We don't want to slow down the service, but if given a few minutes to find the Scriptures in your personal Bible, people begin to build a new level of awareness for the comprehensiveness of Scripture and where a specific reading fits into the larger, unfolding story.

Pick out a 30-day period of time. Every other day, replace traditional meal prayers with a prayer spoken from your heart, invoking the blessings of Jesus and praying in His name. Bishop Robert Barron, auxiliary Bishop of the Archdiocese of Los Angeles and host of "Word on Fire," identifies one specific lesson that Catholics could learn from our Evangelical brothers and sisters in Christ. "They can teach us to be more comfortable with the name of Jesus."[32]

Not sure you can do this? I can identify with you. I stumbled for many miles before I hit a good stride. Perhaps a little encouragement from St. Jerome will help. He said, "The Scriptures are shallow enough for a babe to come and drink without fear of drowning and deep enough for a theologian to dive in without ever touching the bottom."[33]

There is one more promise from the Bible that should be a great encouragement for you. The Prophet Isaiah declared the following promise from God: "So is my word that goes out from my mouth: It will not return to me empty but will accomplish what I desire and achieve the purpose for which I sent it" (Isaiah 55:11). When the Word of God enters your heart, trust the Lord has a purpose. Also, trust that the power of the Holy Spirit will help you achieve it. Once persuaded by the Holy Spirit, we become persuasive in sharing and witnessing to the difference Christ makes in our life and in the world.

Reflection

1. Studying our faith and reading Scripture is like jumping on a merry-go-round. There is no one right place to jump on; the important thing is that you get on and get going! There will be questions, doubts, and challenges along the way. What can you do to move toward Christ over the next 30 days?

2. Making changes in our life can be tough. Consider the following approach: Focus on one change at a time. Don't expect to get it right the first time. Work to do a little more good than you did yesterday and a little less bad than the day before. We are all works in-progress. What change do you want to start with? What change would make the biggest impact on those around you?

9

What Puts Us at Risk
Considering Our Great History
and a Great Temptation

I have surrendered my free will to the years of accumulated habits and the past deeds of my life have already marked out a path which threatens to imprison my future. My bad habits must be destroyed and new furrows prepared for good seed. ~Og Mandino

Having applied spiritual first aid, stop and check your pulse. Take a moment with anyone with whom you are working and see how they are doing. This can be an exhilarating experience for some and hard work for others. Rest assured that additional help is on the way. We also need to stop and thank God for His present grace and mercy, healing, and hope. For some, you might be applying first aid to a spiritual paper cut or even a broken bone. For others, it is more serious—a heart attack or even full resuscitation of flat-lined faith. God's grace and mercy are always greater than our turmoil and pain.

Understanding how we get to a point of needing first aid

is important. We need to understand any risk factors so we can prevent infection and avoid contact with viruses in our environment. We'll want to have this information for ourselves, but we'll also want to put the appropriate ointments in our spiritual first aid bag so that we can minister to those around us.

If you are like me, it's much easier and safer to help someone else. But we all need to keep a critical truth in mind. Think back to your last flight or your favorite airline mystery movie. Before take-off, passengers are always walked through the safety talk. When the oxygen mask drops, people are directed to help whom? Many of us think about helping others first, but the stewardess is right. We need to put the oxygen mask on ourselves first. We can't help anyone if we are dead. Taking care of ourselves spiritually is the best thing we can do for our family, friends, and community.

The risk factors are any elements, beliefs, and actions that can become stumbling blocks in our walk with the Lord—anything that keeps us from getting caught up in Christ as the foundation of our faith. My risk factors as a long time Catholic might be different from yours. I hope this review of my risk factors will help you better understand yours and those of your family and friends. Over the years, I have come to understand my primary risk factors relate to church history, church impact, and Catholic ego.

The Story of the Church

The Catholic Church traces its roots back to Christ Himself as described in the Book of Acts. Following the development of the Church is fascinating. There are stories of champions, great accomplishments, and martyrs who died for

Christ. Many hospitals and organizations have been founded by the Roman Catholic Church and its ministers. But like all great stories, there are good, bad, and ugly days in the life of the Church. This is not the place for a full review of Church history. It is, however, the place to recognize the prominent role of the Roman Catholic Church throughout the history of the world and into present times.

I liken the story of the Church to the story of the Ford Motor Company. The Ford Motor Company began making cars in 1903. The company became the first to produce large numbers of motorized vehicles. Ford quickly became the world's largest and most famous of the early car manufacturers. Still today, the Ford name is synonymous with cars and trucks. By 1909, there were calls for new models and new colors. Up until that time, every Ford was painted black because black paint took the least amount of time to dry. Henry Ford didn't want to slow down his production process to watch paint dry. During a meeting in 1909, Henry Ford declared that "customers can have a car painted any color they want as long as it's black."[34] The demand for change persisted. Later that year, the company sold the first Model T— painted red.[35]

Like the Ford Motor Company, one could argue that the Roman Catholic Church was the first prominent organization dedicated to the Christian faith. Like auto companies that followed Ford, new denominations would emerge from the Roman Catholic Church. For example, Martin Luther didn't grab his hammer to start the Protestant reformation. He nailed his 95 Thesis to Wittenberg castle to bring light to issues within his Catholic church with hopes of seeing change. In simple terms, he would be the first to call for a car of a different color.

Luther's protest catalyzed the Protestant Reformation. Over time, the story of the Catholic church would include other challenging issues and dark times. These dark times, including the ongoing sexual abuse crisis, can manifest as a significant stumbling block. People, me included, wrestle to make sense of the issues. If we are not careful, our faith life can become consumed by issues in the church. In doing so, we run the risk of being caught up in the church versus being caught up in Christ.

Understanding church history helps us keep events, crises, and our personal experiences with the church in perspective. I believe we benefit from having a solid understanding of church history, including a good understanding of our Jewish heritage. It is foundational to the Christian faith. These stories illuminate the unfolding story of God's creation, and how Christ is redeeming the world.

The Impact of the Church

The record of church history includes the development of specific theological positions, doctrinal statements, and liturgical traditions. It is fascinating to study the different teachings of the Catholic Church and how they compare to the teachings of other Christian denominations. Such an investigation reveals elements of church: the way we worship, how we feel about church authority, the role of intercessory prayer, etc. We could make a long list of similarities and differences.

There is great majesty and ceremony in the Catholic Church. Some of my closest moments to Jesus Christ have come while engaged in the sacred elements of Mass. We would be hard-pressed to identify a faith tradition with more elements of church. We would also be equally challenged to find another tradition with more potential distractions. If we are not careful, we can get caught up in the elements of church that can distract us from the qualities of Christ.

Throughout the book, we've examined five qualities of Christ. We have considered the peace of Christ, the powerful partnership in which believers can invest, and the benefits of a godly perspective. We have also considered pure thoughts and deferring to the teachings of Christ to avoid the consequences of bad thinking. We have also looked at how the Holy Spirit persuades our hearts and minds and then often works through us to persuade others.

Looking back, I now see the impact the church had on my life. I spent many years caught up in the elements of church and not the qualities of Christ. Mike, one of the many people who helped me pull this book together, captured this reality in his life: "I had an allegiance to the church before I had an allegiance to Christ." Elements of church can bring us closer to Christ, but they can also put us at risk, if we are not careful to keep sacred things in proper perspective.

Not only can church impact our individual relationship with Christ, it can also impact our relationship with other people, and how we share Christ with those around us. When I speak with others inside my faith tradition, I find it easy to connect on the elements of church: the substance of the liturgy and the sacredness of Mass. We may share specific sacraments that have special meaning for each of us.

However, when I speak with people who are not of the Catholic faith, connecting on the elements of church is challenging, if not impossible. Some may not be connected to any faith tradition and have no experience inside an organized worship experience, so we find no common ground on any element of church. Others may be experienced with community worship, but we might differ on specific traditions like the celebration of communion. I have also had conversations with people who attend my Catholic Church but are not engaged in the Mass. For example, there are young people who attend Mass only because they are expected to, but they are not engaged. In all these situations, attempting to connect with people on the elements of church have left them uninspired and me frustrated.

Recognizing the difference between elements of church and qualities of Christ equipped me to have more meaningful interactions. Rather than focusing on the elements of church, focusing on the qualities of Christ lead to more comfortable interactions and sustained conversations where I had the opportunity to share Christ.

Dagmar was the first to help me learn this great lesson. I was worried about the faith of our three sons. They had stopped attending church, and I wasn't sure if they still believed in God. One day, I was in the workshop and Eli stopped in. After taking care of some yardwork, he asked me to listen to a new country music song, entitled "Beer With Jesus" by artist Thomas Rhett.

When the song stopped playing, I praised God and thanked my son. He still believed! We spent a wonderful moment, caught up in Christ.

Dagmar and I had a similar experience with our youngest son, Ehren, and Naomi, our wonderful daughter-in-law. They had settled in a large city five hours north of us. A few weeks prior to a scheduled visit, I heard there was going to be a play in town honoring the 500-year anniversary of the Reformation. I was studying this time of church history, and

I knew Dagmar would enjoy the show. I wasn't sure the kids would attend but asked anyway. They agreed to go! "Luther on Trial" was a wonderful production. It ended with the verse from 1 John 4:4: "You belong to God, children, and you have conquered them, for the one who is in you is greater than the one who is in the world."

On the way home, the kids admitted that they only agreed to go because they didn't want to disappoint us. "But, you know," Ehren said, "I am glad we went. If I had known what this was going to be about, I would have read up on the story." We talked about Christ the whole way home. I'll never forget that evening! We would not have been able to connect with the kids around the elements of church, but we were able to connect around the qualities of Christ.

As I listen to people, they often express a need or a problem. I've discovered that they often tie into one or more of the qualities of Christ. We may not always be able to connect with people on the elements of church, but I believe we can always find communion with people around the qualities of Christ. This approach fits with our focus on spiritual first-aid and connecting with people who currently know Christ and those who do not.

Catholic Ego

I was born into a wonderful and loving Catholic family. I don't have twelve siblings, but I have three older sisters! We were faithful church goers. I attended Catholic schools for twelve years. I was an altar boy and received all the prescribed Sacraments. I didn't read my Bible. I didn't feel the need to; I was Catholic. I couldn't quote scripture. I didn't think I needed to; I was Catholic. I couldn't give evidence for God. I wasn't taught this in Catholic school. I remember people asking me if I was Christian and I proudly proclaimed, "No. I am Catholic." I didn't know what I was saying.

I accepted Jesus Christ as my personal Lord and Savior at the age of 38. As I grew in my faith, I came to understand that I had been suffering from what I call my Catholic ego. Looking back, my simple identity with the Catholic Church kept me organized around the elements of church, its structures and rules, but disconnected from the qualities of Christ. This was not a feature of the content but an unintended result of the process. My teachers and our parish priests had every intention of schooling us in the ways of God while teaching us the ways of the church. But I became distracted by the elements of church and struggled to connect with the qualities of Christ.

Moved by the Holy Spirit and encouraged by a team of spiritual mentors and guides, I set out on a journey to study the Word, to understand the basics of the Catholic faith, and to nurture my personal relationship with Jesus Christ.

No one likes to have their faith questioned, especially those suffering from Catholic ego. I was blessed by people who were patient with me and respected my identity with the Catholic Church. I engaged in critical conversations with people inside and outside the Catholic Church, and even inside and outside the Christian faith. I praise God for revealing Himself to me and persuading me of the truth about Jesus Christ. I have come to identify with a declaration made often by Dr. Frank Turek. "People don't think Christianity is true. They are talked out of it. You know why they are talked out of it? Because they've never been talked into it."[36]

I remain connected with my parish community and look

forward to worship. Getting caught up in Christ has enhanced by experience of the Mass. I also continue to supplement my faith walk, overcome any inertia that can develop over time, and to remain aware of any risk factors jeopardizing my walk with the Lord. Reading God's Word has been indispensable as I have deepened my personal relationship with Jesus and enjoyed His peace, power, perspective, pure thoughts, and persuasion.

Reflection

1. For many people, "church" impacts how they organize their weekly schedule, their social relationships, volunteer time, and, to some degree, their finances. These elements of church can be meaningful and help in their walk with Jesus Christ. They can also serve, unintentionally, as a distraction. Are there modifications you need to make to ensure you are getting caught up in Christ and not just the elements of church?

2. Can you identify with the description of "Catholic ego" or see any spiritual inertia that has developed in your life?

3. What personal beliefs are you aware of that do not line up with church teaching? What would you do if you discovered that specific church teaching conflicted with biblical truth?

10

A Trajectory Decision
Real Life Outcomes, Real World Implications

Is it possible that the ideas we hold to be true could actually contribute to a false view of reality? Each of us tends to think we see things as they are, that we are objective. But this is not the case. We see the world, not as it is, but as we are—or, as we are conditioned to see it. When we open our mouths to describe what we see, we in effect describe ourselves, our perceptions, our paradigms. ~*Stephen R. Covey*

As I finish writing this book, the world is celebrating the 50th anniversary of the first moon landing. The Eagle landed on July 20, 1969. Astronaut Buzz Aldrin piloted the lunar module that delivered Neil Armstrong to the surface of the moon. Think of the Apollo 11 rocket as they counted down to take-off. If the ship had been two degrees off target at launch, the ship would have missed its target and the moon. And, if the lunar module had been two degrees off target as it made its final approach to the moon, it would have missed its target but still hit the moon. The trajectory of the ship at launch was critical to mission success.

We make certain decisions that set the course for our life, dictate outcomes and impact how we experience the world and how the world experiences us. Choosing to love God freely and accepting Jesus Christ into our hearts is a trajectory decision. Choosing to withhold our love from God and denying Christ's kingship in our heart is also a trajectory decision.

The world conditions us to see differences: race, religion, sex, gender, ethnicity, citizenship. The list seems to be growing, along with tensions between groups focused on their primary identity. In God, we all find a common identity as children of the Master Creator. As God is removed from our society, so goes recognition of God the Creator and our common heritage. This leaves groups to fight for their own identity, worldview, and objectives with little incentive to find common ground.

Grounded in our primary identity as children of God, Christians see common ground with those around us. Some may be closer to Christ and others a world away, but we are all brothers and sisters in Christ. In the five qualities of Christ, we find common human drives and outcomes that everyone seeks. Both believers and non-believers alike seek peace, powerful partnerships to achieve desired change, perspectives, and pure thoughts that help them avoid bad thinking. Within their given worldview, people are persuaded of certain ideas and then find themselves promoting their beliefs and values to others. The differences are in who or what lie at the heart of anyone's spirituality, their worldview, and how they pursue desired outcomes. Make no mistake, the outcomes can be drastically different.

Relationship with Self

M. Scott Peck begins his book, *The Road Less Traveled,* with a powerful lesson.

> Life is difficult. This is a great truth, one of the greatest truths. It is a great truth because once we truly see this truth, we transcend it. Once we truly know that life is difficult-once we truly understand and accept it—then life is no longer difficult. Because once it is accepted, the fact that life is difficult no longer matters.[37]

Accepting this truth is a trajectory decision. If we, instead, think things will be easy for us, expecting only simple challenges with simple solutions, life lived pain-free, with others bearing responsibility for our situations, feelings, and decisions, we wake each morning with a sense of entitlement, somehow thinking that the world owes us.

As we get caught up in Christ, we gain a better perspective on the evidence for the truth that life is difficult. Things are going to happen to us. The company we work for may shut down and put us out of work. Our best friend may join the military and be gone for an entire year. We may find out that our romantic partner has been cheating on us. We might break our leg in the first football game of the season. Our cousin might be killed in a drive-by shooting. We might get hit by a drunk driver or be diagnosed with a terminal illness.

Although life is difficult, there are good things that happen to us too. We might get that professional acting break we've been looking for. We might win a new car in the church raffle. We might meet that someone special after years of being alone. We may reunite with an estranged sibling.

Our child might get clean from drugs or break their gambling addiction. Our house might be spared from a severe storm. We might experience an unexplained healing.

How we make sense of the world around us impacts how we respond to the events that happen to us and around us. As we get caught up in Christ, we find strength to keep going during tough times and encouragement to remain hope-filled during desperate times. Can you identify times in your life when you faced challenges and yet were hope-filled? Did you make different decisions during these times versus times when you were distraught and had lost hope? How we receive and understand the good things that happen to us is also telling. Believers receive the good things as blessings from God, and our humbled heart beats with gratitude. Others may have a mindset of "I deserved that" and demand more. Have you noticed that demanding people are seldom content and have a hard time finding peace?

Christ-enabled changes show up in our life in different ways, one believer to the next. I listen to different music and watch different television programs. I go to different types of movies, and I manage my personal finances much differently. The changes showed up at work and in my recreational time too.

Along with inviting Christ into my life, I also allowed other truth-tellers into my life. Jim, my mentor, and others, helped me develop a teachable spirit. Reading the Bible is a mainstay of this steady diet of truth. This has led to a greater sense of personal responsibility for my actions and self-discipline required to achieve goals.

Our relationship with self is also significantly impacted by our orientation to time. When bad things happen, some people get stuck in the past. When good things happened in the past, some people relive those events over and over again, and stay anchored in the past and miss out on new opportunities. Compare this dynamic with the person who always looks forward. When we get preoccupied with goal setting and are convinced that life will start only when we achieve this goal or that goal, we can get caught up in the future. People can get fixated on the future to the extent they avoid their current situations, responsibilities, and obligations.

The Bible highlights a great lesson here. Do you recall the story of Moses and the burning bush? God gave Moses directions to go to Egypt. We pick up the story in Exodus 3:11-14.

> But Moses said to God, "Who am I that I should go to Pharaoh and bring the Israelites out of Egypt?" God answered: I will be with you; and this will be your sign that I have sent you. When you have brought the people out of Egypt, you will serve God at this mountain. "But," said Moses to God, "if I go to the Israelites and say to them, 'The God of your ancestors has sent me to you,' and they ask me, 'What is his name?' what do I tell them?" God replied to Moses: I am who I am. Then he added: This is what you will tell the Israelites: I AM has sent me to you."

Jesus Christ, the second person of the Holy Trinity, is not the great I will be or the great I was; He is the great I AM! I believe we do well when we strive to stay present-minded. Are there events in your past you have yet to resolve, hard times that still tie up a great deal of your mental energy and impact how you experience the world? Are you keeping the future in proper perspective? There was a time when I was so focused on the future that I missed many moments with those around me. This also prevented me from being a more effective dad and husband. Bill Keane says it best: yesterday is history, tomorrow is a mystery, today is a gift of God, which is why we call it the present.[38]

Relationships with Others

Getting caught up in Christ not only impacts the way we experience the world, but how the world experiences us. We are sons and daughters, siblings, and friends. We are spouses and partners. We parent our children, and sometimes we parent our children and grandchildren in the same house. We engage with co-workers on the job. We interact with strangers at the movie theatres and pursue a relationship with the person who has caught our attention. We care for our loved ones and our loved ones care for us. I am still a work in progress, but I have made positive changes in how I impact those around me. Dagmar and our boys could tell you stories! I am not proud of some of the ways I impacted their lives early on. I thank them for giving me room to grow and change. I thank God for their continued presence in my life.

Our relationship with Christ impacts how we interact with people. Getting caught up in Christ also impacts how we understand our need for community, our connection with people, and our opportunities to help those around us. We live in a world of multiple means of connectivity at the very same time that we are more acquainted with loneliness and isolation. Listen to how John Eldredge describes our need to connect with other people.

Christ wants to do more for us than simply forgive. He wants to restore us. And He then calls those who are being restored to help rescue others. That is why God calls together small communities of the heart— to fight for one another and for the hearts of those who have not yet been set free. We hear each other's stories. We discover each other's glories. We learn to walk with God together. We pray for each other's healing. We cover each other's back. Sure, Jesus spoke to the masses. But he lived in a little platoon, a small fellowship of friends and allies. We find ourselves in a love Story set in the midst of a life-and-death battle. Just look around you. Look at the casualties strewn across the field. The lost souls, the broken hearts, the captives. We must take this battle seriously. This is a war—a battle for the human heart. And we have reached the moment where we must find our courage and rise up to recover our hearts and fight for the hearts of others. There is nothing more exhilarating, nothing more profoundly beautiful, than to rescue the life of another human being.[39]

Relationship with Ideas

Our quality of life is greatly influenced by our relationship with self, our relationship with others, and our relationship with ideas. Ideas are important because they impact how we understand the world, and they influence the decisions we make on a daily basis. Ideas circulating through our culture are important because they have this same impact on large numbers of people. Christians are called to be salt and light to the world (Matthew 5:13-16). This, in part, means that we are to seek to understand ideas from God's perspective and speak truth, with great love, into the hearts and minds of those around us.

Let's take an idea to see how this works. We could choose from among many ideas circulating through our culture today—global warming, border security, free speech, one-world government, one-world religion, the Rapture of the Church. However, it would be hard to find an idea that is impacting our culture more than sex and human sexuality. Could we find an area of our culture where sex and sexuality has not exerted a strong influence? More than any other idea, the intensity of the conversations and debates surrounding human sexuality can leave us confused, conflicted, and, often times, quiet.

St. Paul teaches us an important truth about the Word of God. "All scripture is inspired by God and is useful for teaching, for refutation, for correction, and for training in righteousness so that one who belongs to God may be competent, equipped for every good work" (2 Timothy 3: 16-17). If Christ is unable to provide answers to our most challenging questions, what value is there in His teaching? If the Bible is unable to provide relevant and coherent explanations for our most difficult situations, where is relevance in the Word? We don't need a Messiah who is right when we are right. We need a Messiah who is right when we are wrong.

I recently had the opportunity to visit with a young person who was interviewing for a position at the university where I work. After speaking for a short time, the young person announced that he had completed sex reassignment surgery. Female by birth, the young person now identifies as a man. He asked me how he would be received in the community.

I struggled for years in an industry that is decidedly supportive of the LGBTQ+ agenda. I wondered if there was a consistent biblical view on human sexuality and sexual expression. Could I love my fellow brothers and sisters in Christ while not celebrating their worldview and personal choices? Could I arrive at a place where I was confident sharing my faith with people who subscribed to different worldviews and held different values?

I found clarity in the teaching of Dr. David Anderson, Senior Pastor of Bridgeway Community Church. Dr. Anderson came to the campus where I worked. He shared many lessons with us about Christianity and diversity and connecting with people who share different worldviews. The lesson that has meant the most to me was his lesson about the safety-celebration continuum.

When the young person asked me how he would be received by our community, I shared the following with him. I told him that we valued the safety-celebration continuum. Along with others, I believed he and all people deserve physical and psychological safety, but not everyone, including myself, would celebrate his worldview and choices. I went on to share with him that I believe God created us male and female, and our sexuality, like our race or ethnicity, is sacred. They are both determined by God.

We went on to enjoy what I thought was an open, honest, and sincere exchange about our values and the basis for our different worldviews. The conversation ended with a genuine handshake. Later that evening, I saw him again. He thanked me for my honesty and transparency, informing me that he had not heard that perspective before.

Today, more than ever, the biblical worldview often

stands in contrast with ideas circulating in our culture. When we hear cries for diversity and inclusiveness, Christians need to feel confident in sharing ideas from the biblical worldview. Issues centered around sex may be front and center in our culture today and perhaps even in our individual lives. As a married man, I am conscious of the commitment I made to Dagmar. When I said "yes" to her, I said "no" to all the millions of other women around the world. But it's important to keep in mind that all the decisions we make and the outcomes we pursue bring us closer to or move us further away from the will of God.

As we've discussed, many voices are shouting at us in our culture today. Have you also noticed that the messages seem to be emotionally infused and lacking critical thought? We are encouraged to think in three and four minute bursts which often leaves little room for discerning relevance, coherence, and truth. Getting caught up in Christ helps us seek godly wisdom, and surrounding ourselves with other truth-tellers helps us think critically about our situations and choices.

In Christ, I find relevant and coherent perspectives on ideas that are unique from any other worldview. And each day I am more and more convinced that we have a beautiful story to tell, a story that brings hope and healing to a hurting world.

Relationship with God

Getting caught up in Christ informs and equips us to enhance our relationship with ourselves, other people, ideas, and God Himself. Each time we recite the Apostles Creed, we profess great truths. Each time we attend church, we proclaim them.

I believe in God, the Father almighty, creator of heaven and earth. I believe in Jesus Christ, His only Son, our Lord. He was conceived by the power of the Holy Spirit and born of the Virgin Mary. He suffered under Pontius Pilate, was crucified, died, and was buried. He descended into hell. On the third day He rose again in fulfilment of the Scriptures. He ascended into heaven and is seated at the right hand of the Father. He will come again to judge the living and the dead.

In making this profession, we acknowledge the nature of God the Father, and Christ the Son. The third person of the Trinity, the Holy Spirit, is mentioned later in the Creed. This understanding of who God is also helps us to clarify who we are and to whom we are accountable. From 1947 to 2005, Billy Graham spoke openly about sin, judgment, and the Good News of the Gospel. The Graham crusades were often held in football stadiums and broadcast on national television in prime time. Can you imagine that happening today?

As God is removed from our society and from our hearts, so goes the realization that each of us will, at an appointed time, bow before the Almighty God and be judged. The Bible tells us that "As I live, says the Lord, every knee shall bend before me, and every tongue shall give praise to God" (Romans 14:11). By whose standards will we be judged—God's laws or our ideas and opinions?

I remember the first time I grasped the full weight of Hebrews 10:31: "It is a fearful thing to fall into the hands of the living God." It was at that moment when I also grasped the full effect of the qualities of Christ. How can I stand before a righteous God? I cannot. No matter how good I try to be, I have debts that need to be paid. Enter Christ, my Hero, my Savior, and my God.

Relationship with Christ

I've been making the case that getting caught up in Christ impacts how we experience the world and how the world experiences us. When I stop to think about what my life would be like without Christ, I get a sick feeling in my stomach. Every once in a while, I'll have a conversation with someone who knew me in my earlier years. When I only believed that Jesus was the Messiah, I acted one way. When I started to believe in Jesus as my personal Lord and Savior, I acted in a different way. That has made all the difference. Christ has made all the difference.

> Amazing Grace, how sweet the sound
> That saved a wretch like me
> I once was lost, but now am found
> 'Twas blind but now I see
> 'Twas Grace that taught my heart to fear
> And Grace, my fears relieved
> How precious did that grace appear
> The hour I first believed
> ~*Amazing Grace*

Our experience with the grace of God is directly related to the degree to which we know and acknowledge what occupies our heart, and the level to which we recognize God's ways and His will for our life.

I exhort you to check the pulse of your faith life to determine what or whom lies at the heart of your spirituality.

There will undoubtably be questions and uncertainties but keep in mind that we are engaging in spiritual first aid. There will be opportunities for advanced care. We need to start by answering the essential questions: Who is Jesus? What difference does Jesus make in our life?

The story of the apostle John provides us a beautiful picture of the full experience of Christ. John was with Jesus at the table of the Last Supper (John 13:23). John was present at the Crucifixion, and Jesus commended His mother Mary, to John's care (John 19: 26). John was the first apostle to arrive at the tomb on Easter Sunday (John 20:4). He was also the first to recognize Jesus when Jesus appeared to the disciples after the resurrection (John 21:7). John was "the one whom Jesus loved" (John 13:23; John 19:26; and John 21: 7).

One of the most tender scenes of the New Testament is recorded in John 13:25. The image is presented in nearly every painting of the Lord's Last Supper. This scene of John leaning against the chest of Christ is a captivating picture of the full humanity of Jesus, His approachability, and His eagerness to have a personal connection with those He loves. Imagine what it must have been like for John to hear the heartbeat of the Living God! When we hear the voice of Jesus, we are changed forever! Reflect on this the next time you are in church and approaching the Lord's Table.

John was also chosen by Jesus to receive the revelation of Christ recorded in the Book of Revelation.

I, John, your brother, who share with you the distress, the kingdom, and the endurance we have in Jesus, found myself on the island called Patmos because I proclaimed God's word and gave testimony to Jesus. I was caught up in spirit on the Lord's day and heard behind me a voice as loud as a trumpet, which said, "Write on a scroll what you see and send it to the seven churches: to Ephesus, Smyrna, Pergamum, Thyatira, Sardis, Philadelphia, and Laodicea." Then I turned to see whose voice it was that spoke to me, and when I turned, I saw seven gold lampstands and in the midst of the lampstands one like a son of man, wearing an ankle-length robe, with a gold sash around his chest. The hair of his head was as white as white wool or as snow, and his eyes were like a fiery flame. His feet were like polished brass refined in a furnace, and his voice was like the sound of rushing water. In his right hand he held seven stars. A sharp two-edged sword came out of his mouth, and his face shone like the sun at its brightest. When I caught sight of him, I fell down at his feet as though dead. He touched me with his right hand and said, "Do not be afraid. I am the first and the last, the one who lives. Once I was dead, but now I am alive forever and ever" (Revelation 1:1-17).

John experienced a personal relationship with Christ. He also experienced the full glory of Christ. Intimacy and awe! This is the same Jesus who longs for a personal relationship with you. A thief comes only to steal and slaughter and destroy; Jesus came so that you might have life and have it more abundantly (John 10:10). Jesus longs for you to be caught up in Him. For you see, Jesus is already caught up in you!

Reflection

1. Consider asking God to replace your greatest need and overcome your greatest fear. How would that change the way you experience the world?

2. Reflect on your key relationships. Who is part of your current platoon, as described by Eldredge? Would you benefit from making some changes here?

3. Reflect on the ideas that exert a significant influence on your worldview. How closely do they line up with the full message of the Good News of Christ?

Application and Discussion

We've concluded our application of spiritual first aid for believers and seekers. This last section offers you exercises for individual assessment and the first application of advanced care. Our walk with Christ is dynamic! Our experience ebbs and flows with the seasons of our life. Think of your life as represented by a line graph spanning birth to earthly death. There are horizontal events that we can expect: early childhood experiences, adolescence, young adulthood, work-life experiences, the loss of loved ones, etc. These are developmental markers that delineate our journey. Because they can be anticipated, we can prepare for them.

There are also vertical events that surprise us: health crisis, accidents, world events, unexpected loss of income, parents experiencing loss of children, etc. Though common to humanity, each of us experience different vertical events. Because they cannot be anticipated, it is hard to prepare for them.

Our lives are a journey. With each bend in the road, we do well to reflect and engage in spiritual self-assessment. The following exercises, designed for both individual and group study, will help you assess your current relationship with Christ and your experiences with the five qualities of Christ. The assessments also include recommendations. The recommendations are designed to help you create a prescription for advanced spiritual care.

Share your experiences, your struggles, and success stories by logging on to www.CaughtupinChrist.com. Tell us your experiences and how God is working in your life and in the lives of those to whom you are ministering. The grace of the Lord Jesus Christ and the love of God and the fellowship of the Holy Spirit be with all of you (2 Cor. 13:13).

1. Pursuing Peace

A. Reflect on your current situation and assess your sense of peace. Using the scales below, place an "X" on the scale that best represents where you are currently. There are multiple scales so that you can assess the different areas of your life. Your sense of peace may be the same across the board. This exercise may also reveal that you are experiencing different levels of peace in different areas of your life.

Area: _____ Date: _____

Peace
Sources of stress, have resources and confidence to manage
Sources of stress, have resources but lack confidence to manage
Sources of stress, lack resources and confidence to manage but still have hope
Sources of stress, lack resources and confidence to manage and am losing hope
Sources of stress, lack resources and confidence to manage and have lost hope
I am done.

Area: _____ Date: _____

Peace
Sources of stress, have resources and confidence to manage
Sources of stress, have resources but lack confidence to manage
Sources of stress, lack resources and confidence to manage but still have hope
Sources of stress, lack resources and confidence to manage and am losing hope
Sources of stress, lack resources and confidence to manage and have lost hope
I am done.

B. To whom or what are you currently turning to find peace in your life?

_____

_____

_____

Sometimes when we stop to assess our situations, we find that our answers have become part of our problem. If change is needed and if you are at a point where you want to make a change, take a moment to take inventory of the people and resources around you who can help. There are resources to help you begin reading the Bible so that you can tune into God and the peace that comes from a personal relationship with Jesus Christ. Identify partners to help you attain more peace in your life. Peace partners can join you in shared prayer.

Jesus tells us that "Whenever two or more are gathered in my name, there I will be" (Matthew 18:20). This is not just a cute idea. I believe that Jesus gave us this instruction for three specific reasons: First, to reduce our tendency toward self-reliance and social isolation. Second, to encourage us to speak our faith publicly. Keep in mind what Jesus said in Matthew 10:32-33: "Whoever acknowledges me before others, I will also acknowledge before my Father in heaven. But whoever disowns me before others, I will disown before my Father in heaven." This feeds into the third reason. In multiple texts, St. Paul illustrates how the righteousness with God is revealed from "faith to faith" (Romans 1:17). When we share our faith with others and allow others to share their faith with us, we activate this faith dynamic.

C. Committing Bible verses to memory. In the space below, write down Bible verses that have struck you in a special way. Rehearse them daily until they roll off your tongue. You'll find them a great value during sleepless nights and when someone in your life needs encouragement.

_____

_____

_____

2. Pursuing a Powerful Partnership

A. Reflect on your current situation and assess your sense of power. In this context, we will define power as the ability to affect a desired outcome in a specific area of our life. For example, this might be power to improve our relationships, to increase effectiveness at work, or overcome an addiction. Using the scales below, place an "X" on the scale that best represents where you are currently. There are multiple scales so that you can assess the different areas of your life. Your sense of power may be the same across the board. This exercise may also help you see that you are experiencing different levels of power in the different areas of your life.

Area: _____   Date: _____

Possess power to effect change in earthly matters; rely on Christ's power with
    spiritual matters
Making positive strides to effect change in earthly matters; asking God to
    help me leverage Christ's power over spiritual matters
Lack power to effect change in earthly matters; unaware of current
    spiritual matters in my life
Giving up on finding positive power in earthly matters; walking away from
    God and lack faith that Christ can will help me in spiritual matters
Effect change by disempowering others; have made deals with Satan related
    to spiritual matters

Area: _____   Date: _____

Possess power to effect change in earthly matters; rely on Christ's power with
    spiritual matters
Making positive strides to effect change in earthly matters; asking God to
    help me leverage Christ's power over spiritual matters
Lack power to effect change in earthly matters; unaware of current
    spiritual matters in my life

Giving up on finding positive power in earthly matters; walking away from
God and lack faith that Christ can will help me in spiritual matters
Effect change by disempowering others; have made deals with Satan related
to spiritual matters

B. To whom or what are you currently turning to access power
in your life?

_____

_____

_____

Sometimes when we stop to assess our situations, we find
that our answers have become part of our problem. If change
is needed and if you are at a point where you want to make
a change, take a moment to take inventory of the people and
resources around you who can help. There are also resources
to help you begin studying the Bible so that you can tune into
God and the power that comes from a personal relationship
with Jesus Christ. Identify partners to help you attain more
power in your life. Power partners can join you in shared
prayer, as well.

C. Committing Bible verses to memory. In the space
below, write down Bible verses that have struck you in a special way. Rehearse them daily until they roll off your tongue.
You'll find them a great value during sleepless nights and
when someone in your life needs encouragement to find positive sources of power in earthly and spiritual matters.

_____

_____

_____

3. Pursuing a Godly Perspective

A. Reflect on your current situation and assess your sense of perspective. Using the scales below, place an "X" on the scale that best represents where you are currently. There are multiple scales so that you can assess the different areas of your life. Your sense of perspective may be the same across the board. This exercise may also help you see that you may have a godly perspective in some areas of your life, and not others.

Area: _____ Date: _____

Regularly seek out God's perspective and act on His will
Aware that I need to seek out God's perspective and clarity on His will
Unaware of God's perspective and that He declares His will through the Bible and ministry of the Holy Spirit
Troubled by God's perspective and more comfortable with my perspective and other secular positions
God is not involved in my life and Christ is no savior; what I think is what really matters

Area: _____ Date: _____

Regularly seek out God's perspective and act on His will
Aware that I need to seek out God's perspective and clarity on His will
Unaware of God's perspective and that He declares His will through the Bible and ministry of the Holy Spirit
Troubled by God's perspective and more comfortable with my perspective and other secular positions
God is not involved in my life and Christ is no savior; what I think is what really matters

B. To whom or what are you currently turning to get perspective?

_____

_____

_____

Sometimes when we stop to assess our situations, we find that our answers have become part of our problem. If change is needed and if you are at a point where you want to make a change, take a moment to take inventory of the people and resources around you who can help. There are also resources to help you begin studying the Bible so that you can tune into God's perspective. Identify partners to help you attain a more godly perspective. Perspective partners can join you in shared prayer, as well.

C. Committing Bible verses to memory. In the space below, write down Bible verses that have struck you in a special way. Rehearse them daily until they roll off your tongue. You'll find them a great value during sleepless nights and when someone in your life needs a godly perspective.

_____

_____

_____

4. Pursuing Pure Thoughts

A. Reflect on your current situation and assess your purity of thought. Using the scales below, place an "X" on the scale that best represents where you are currently. There are multiple scales so that you can assess the different areas of your life. Your thought patterns may be the same across the board. This exercise may also help you see that you have bad thinking in some areas of your life and good thoughts in others.

Area: _____ Date: _____

Regularly assess my thoughts to ensure they are based on truth and God's Word

Aware that I tend toward negative thinking; working to transform my mind according to God's Word

Do not question the quality of my thought patterns; unaware that God speaks into our lives

Troubled by God's Word on things in my life; more and more comfortable with secular views

God is not involved in my life; Christ is no savior; truth is what I say it is; I define good and bad

Area: _____ Date: _____

Regularly assess my thoughts to ensure they are based on truth and God's Word

Aware that I tend toward negative thinking; working to transform my mind according to God's Word

Do not question the quality of my thought patterns; unaware that God speaks into our lives

Troubled by God's Word on things in my life; more and more comfortable with secular views

God is not involved in my life; Christ is no savior; truth is what I say it is; I define good and bad

B. To whom or what are you currently turning to determine if your thoughts are good or bad?

_____

_____

_____

Sometimes when we stop to assess our situations, we find that our answers have become part of our problem. If change is needed and if you are at a point where you want to make a change, take a moment to take inventory of the people and resources around you who can help. There are also resources to help you begin studying the Bible so that you can tune into truth and good thoughts based on God's Word. Identify partners to help you attain pure thoughts. Pure thought partners can join you in shared prayer, as well.

C. Committing Bible verses to memory. In the space below, write down Bible verses that have struck you in a special way. Rehearse them daily until they roll off your tongue. You'll find them a great value when you are face to face with bad thoughts and when someone in your life needs truth based on God's word.

_____

_____

_____

5. Pursuing Persuasion

A. Reflect on your current situation and assess how comfortable you are with the Good News of Jesus Christ and how persuasively you share the Gospel. Using the scales below, place an "X" on the scale that best represents where you are currently. There are multiple scales so that you can assess the different areas of your life. You may feel confident in some areas and not so confident in others.

Area: _____   Date: _____

Unashamed of the Gospel and confident sharing the Good News with everyone
Unashamed of the Gospel and confident sharing the Good News with believers
Unashamed of the Gospel but nervous about sharing the Good News at all
Firm in my personal faith but still have doubts about many things, afraid
  to share with others
New believer in Christ and not even sure what it means to share the Good News

Area: _____   Date: _____

Unashamed of the Gospel and confident sharing the Good News with everyone
Unashamed of the Gospel and confident sharing the Good News with believers
Unashamed of the Gospel but nervous about sharing the Good News at all
Firm in my personal faith but still have doubts about many things, afraid
    to share with others
New believer in Christ and not even sure what it means to share the Good News

B. This can be a most intimidating element of being a follower of Christ. Christ calls us and assures us that the Holy Spirit will help us. "But you will receive power when the Holy Spirit comes on you; and you will be my witnesses in Jerusalem, and in all Judea and Samaria, and to the ends of the earth" (Acts 1:8). It may be helpful to break this down into three parts: receive, share, and witness. When we receive enough, we will naturally begin to share what we've received. As we share this Good News, the Lord equips us and, before you know it, we are witnessing to believers and then to nonbelievers. The first step is to begin a personal relationship with Jesus Christ and pray that God will bless you with spiritual gifts, healing, deliverance, and a deep and true repentance. Identify persuasive partners to help you along this path.

C. Committing Bible verses to memory. In the space below, write down Bible verses that have struck you in a special way. Rehearse them daily until they roll off your tongue. You'll find them a great value when you are face to face with bad thoughts and when someone in your life wants to hear the Good News of Jesus Christ.

_____

_____

_____

Notes

1 Marannis, David. *When Pride Still Mattered: A Life of Vince Lombardi.* https://masterworks.com/2016/07/this-is-a-football/ (July 13, 2019).

2 https://progressivechristianity.org/the-8-points/ (July 13, 2019).

3 https://www.brainyquote.com/quotes/winston_churchill_111291 (July 13, 2019).

4 Lewis, C.S. *Mere Christianity* (London: Geoffrey Bles, 1952), 55-56.

5 http://vatican2voice.org/92symp/murray.htm (July 13, 2019).

6 Bishop Robert Barron. https://www.youtube.com/watch?v=I8yCkYT50No (July 13, 2019).

7 White, Michael, and Corcoran, Tom. *Rebuilt-The Story of a Catholic Parish* (Notre Dame, Indiana: Ave Maria Press, 2013), 130.

8 https://creation.com/universe-had-a-beginning Web July 13, 2019.

9 http://www.hawking.org.uk/the-beginning-of-time.html (July 13, 2019).

10 Geisler, N., and Turek, F., *I Don't Have Enough Faith to Be an Atheist* (Wheaton, IL: Crossway, 2004), 93.

11 *The God Who Speaks: Tracing the Evidence for Biblical Authority* (DVD). (Tupelo, MS: American Family Studios, 2017).

12 The word "suppressed" was chosen specifically. It relates back to Paul's use of the term in Romans 1:18. "For the wrath of God is revealed from heaven against all ungodliness and unrighteousness of men who suppress the truth in unrighteousness, because that which is known about God is evident within them; for God made it evident to them."

13 Scholars cite evidence that suggests that the Book of Job was the first book record, perhaps as early as 2000-1800 BC. Compare this with the Book of Genesis, which is believed to have been written by Moses around 1400 BC. Cummings, B. and Wubbels, L, Eds. *Founders' Bible, 2nd Edition* (Newbury Park, CA: Shiloh Road Publishers, 2017).

14 St. Augustine's *Confessions.* https://www.crossroadsinitiative.com/media/articles/ourheartisrestlessuntilitrestsinyou/ (July 13, 2019).

15 Price, F., *How Faith Works* (Los Angeles, CA: Faith One Publishing 2001).

16 Gregory. Boyle, *Tattoos on the Heart* (New York: Free Press 2010), 19.

17 DavidJeremiah.org. *Living in the Age of Signs*. The Second Coming of Christ is not Just an Event, It's the Central Theme of the Entire Bible. (August 11, 2019).

18 Ted.com. Rick Warren, "A Life of Purpose." July 2006. Web. April 27, 2019.

19 Jeremiah, David, *Living by Faith: The Book of Romans, Volume 1: God's Righteousness and Man's Rebellion* (San Diego, CA: Turning Point for God, 1999), 56.

20 Strobel, L., *The Case for Christ: A Journalist's Personal Investigation of the Evidence for Jesus* (Grand Rapids, MI: Zondervan, 1998), 198-200.

21 Wellman, Jack. "Historical Evidence of Jesus Christ's Resurrection." https://www.whatchristianswanttoknow.com/historical-evidence-of-jesus-christs-resurrection/ (May 1, 2018).

22 Ibid

23 Frankl, V., *The Doctor and the Soul: From Psychotherapy to Logotherapy*, Quoted on Goodreads.com. (April 27, 2019).

24 Getinvolved.ncsu.edu/organization/satanicstudents (April 27, 2019).

25 Afterschoolsatan.com. (April 27, 2019).

26 Lutz, Donald S. "The Relative Influence of European Writers on Late Eighteenth-Century American Political Thought." *The American Political Science Review*, vol. 78, no. 1, 1984, 189–197. JSTOR, www.jstor.org/stable/1961257 p 92.

27 Jeremiah, David, *Living by Faith: The Book of Romans, Volume 1: God's Righteousness and Man's Rebellion*, (San Diego, CA: Turning Point for God, 1999), 38-39.

28 Koukl, Gregory, *Tactics* (Grand Rapids, MI: Zondervan, 2009), 190.

29 Newell, Williams, R., *Romans Verse by Verse* (Grand Rapids, MI: Kregel Publishing Co., 2003), 345.

30 Loyd-Jones, Martyn, *Romans-Final Perseverance of the Saints-Exposition of Chapter 8:17-39* (Grand Rapids, MI: Zondervan, 1975), 448.

31 www.Dynamic Catholic.org. February 16, 2018. (April 27, 2019).

32 Bishop Robert Barron. https://www.youtube.com/watch?v=I8yCkYT50No Web July 13, 2019.

33 Attributed to St. Jerome. Quoted on Goodreads.com (April 27, 2019).

34 Ford, Henry, *My Life and Work* (New York: Garden City Publishing, 1922), 72.

35 Veer, Jithin, *The Evolution of Color in the American Automotive Industry*. http://www.people.vcu.edu/~djbromle/color-theory/color04/jithin/autocolor.htm (May 7, 2019).
36 Turek, Frank. Included on the introduction to the CrossExamined.com podcast. Web. (April 27, 2019).
37 Peck, M. Scott, *The Road Less Traveled* (New York: Touchstone Book, 1978), 15
38 Keane, Bill. https://www.goodreads.com/quotes/search?q=Yesterday+is+history.+Tomorrow+is+a+mystery.+and+Today+is+a+gift. (September 3, 2019).
39 Eldredge, John. Ransomed Hearts Ministry. https://www.ransomed-heart.com/story/larger-story/rescuing-other (September 2, 2019).

About the Author

Rick Merfeld earned a psychology degree from Luther College and a Master's Degree in Counselor Education from the University of Wisconsin-Platteville. He began his professional career providing mental health services for children, couples, and families. He lived and worked among college students for over 25 years before moving into an executive leadership position with a non-profit organization.

Rick grew up in a loving Catholic home and attended 12 years of Catholic education, followed by four additional years at a Christian college. His spiritual journey continued, and Rick accepted Jesus Christ as Lord and Savior at the age of 38. Rick has been involved with parish leadership and speaks at Christian retreats. Rick and his wife, Dagmar, have been married for 31 years and reside in Iowa. They are parents of three adult sons and have three grandchildren.

Rick can be reached at CaughtupinChrist.com.